THE LAST MON

THE LAST MOUNTAIN

Living With AIDS

JANA GODFREY

with

MERRILYN WILLIAMS

HODDER AND STOUGHTON
LONDON SYDNEY AUCKLAND

Scripture quotations are taken from the HOLY BIBLE,
NEW INTERNATIONAL VERSION, copyright © 1973,
1978, 1984, by the International Bible Society

British Library Cataloguing in Publication Data
A catalogue record for this book
is available from the British Library

ISBN 0-340-58043 7

First published in Great Britain 1993

Published by Hodder and Stoughton,
a division of Hodder and Stoughton Ltd,
Mill Road, Dunton Green, Sevenoaks, Kent TN13 2YA.
Editorial Office: 47 Bedford Square, London WC1B 3DP

Typeset by Hewer Text Composition Services, Edinburgh.
Printed in Great Britain by Clays Ltd, St Ives plc.

This book is dedicated to the memory of Phil,
who was full of fun,
and to Natasha,
who is her father's daughter.

ACKNOWLEDGEMENTS

I would like to acknowledge the love and support of my two families, my own and my in-laws. I would also like to acknowledge with grateful thanks the care and help of the numerous medical staff I met through Phil. They supported our choices and allowed us to live our lives to the full. Thank you to our church families and our friends for all the prayers and practical help they provided. Thanks also to Phil's employers who continued to value him as a scientist in spite of the interruptions to his work caused by his illness. Finally, thank you to Merrilyn who is a good listener and a good writer.

Jana Godfrey

I would like to express my appreciation to all who so generously gave of their time and expertise in helping me to come to a better understanding of the complexities of haemophilia and AIDS in general and, in particular, how these afflictions affected Phil. My thanks must especially be extended to Dr C. R. Rizza, Consultant Physician, Oxford Haemophilia Centre, the Churchill Hospital, Oxford; Dr B. Hirschel, Médecin Adjoint, Division des Maladies Infectieuses, Hôpital Cantonal Universitaire, Genève, Switzerland; Dr Kim Hardy, Assistant Director, and Ms Rita Gloor, Personnel Manager – both of Glaxo IMB, Geneva, Switzerland; and Brigitte Studer, *directrice* of the SIDA organisation in Geneva. I am deeply grateful, also, to Phil's family and friends for their warm hospitality, and for allowing me access to some of their most private and painful experiences – but most of all to Jana and Tash.

Thanks are due, too, to my friends Ros Morrison and Wendy John, to whom I am indebted for their proof-reading of the completed manuscript.

Merrilyn Williams

CONTENTS

1

Lurking in the Shadows

*'And I will put enmity between you and the
woman, and between your offspring and hers;
he will crush your head and you will strike
his heel.'*

Genesis 3:15

'I think everyone with AIDS should go to Hell!'

The words dropped into the air indiscriminately, like
miniature bombshells. Instantly finding a target, they
exploded upon my mind. Painfully. And poignantly.

I winced.

There was no need for me to look up to identify
the speaker. Seated within touching distance in my tiny
sitting-room, he was a regular member of the Bible study
group to whom he'd addressed his remark. Nor, unlike
most of the group, had he the excuse of youth. Though
middle-aged, he frequently spoke without thought.

I wonder how he'd feel, I thought, blinking hard to
disperse the tears that were stinging my eyes, if he knew
that the hospitality he was enjoying was being given by
someone with AIDS?

I glanced around the room at heads bowed earnestly
over the Bible verses being expounded by my husband,
Phil. Young and slight in his T-shirt and jeans, his fair hair
falling in a spiky fringe across his forehead, he was deeply
immersed in the study. We'd only recently taken over

leadership of the group, together with a friend, Richard Mason, but both he and Phil seemed oblivious to the hurt I was experiencing.

The moment everyone had left, later that evening, I took it up with Phil.

'Did you hear what he was saying?'

He was busy scribbling something in a notebook and was obviously preoccupied.

'Hmm? Hear what?' he asked.

'You'd think Christians would show more compassion,' I said and, dashing away the tears in my eyes, began to stack the coffee mugs on a tray.

'Oh that!' Phil looked up and seeing my distress, laid down his jotter, took the tray from my hands and put his arms around me. 'You mustn't let it get to you.'

Fresh tears filled my eyes. 'But, honey, it's so hard . . . I feel everyone is judging us . . . '

Phil raised my chin and looked down at me. 'No one knows,' he said, firmly. 'And it's only ignorance . . . They don't mean to hurt.'

I knew he was right. AIDS was the scourge of the century yet few people even knew what it meant. Acquired Immune Deficiency Syndrome. The name had ugly connotations. Take the word ACQUIRED. Acquired from whom? Or from what? You'd think, to go by most people, that the disease was entirely the result of a depraved or decadent lifestyle. Drugs. Homosexuality. Promiscuity.

Then there was IMMUNE. The virtuous were immune, weren't they? Or so the thinking seemed to go. Did that mean that an absence of AIDS was seen as a sign of righteousness? Of integrity? Clean, decent respectability? Did those who were AIDS-free – to the best of their knowledge – see themselves as commanding the high ground, morally?

And DEFICIENCY? Ah! There was the crux of the matter. Whether openly acknowledged or not, I suspected that those with AIDS were seen as deficient – in more ways than one! Lacking an efficient immune system, weren't they also treated, at times, as if they were lacking some other part of their being? That part that lifts us above the animal kingdom? Leaving them a sort of sub-human species? If the few television pictures and newspaper reports that I'd seen were to be believed, there was a witch-hunt going on in my own country, America. AIDS-sufferers, their spouses and their children were being spurned and vilified by a society driven by fear. In some quarters, hysteria reigned.

Worst of all, however, was the attitude I'd just encountered: that AIDS victims should be cast off as unfit for heaven's salvation, and discarded to eternal damnation. A harsh judgement! And no doubt made unwittingly and unintentionally. Yet could it be construed in any other way?

Fighting the urge to give in to my tears, I put on a brave face for Phil.

'You're prob'ly right,' I admitted. 'I have to learn to ride it . . . '

He hugged me hard, then took the tray out to the kitchen.

Full of love, I watched him go. How did he do it, I wondered? Unlike me, he had evidently shrugged off this latest hurt. But then that was Phil for you! Uncomplicated. Laid back. Always sensitive to others, but never complaining for himself. He turned at the kitchen door. Caught my eye, and winked. Phil. Fun-loving Phil. Just the same now as he was when we'd first met in Richmond, Virginia, USA. Back in 1982. Before this disaster had struck.

*   *   *

'Philip Godfrey.' A pair of pale blue, bespectacled eyes surveyed me calmly as he introduced himself. I'd seen him before in our Sunday School singles group, but with church membership numbering four thousand it wasn't always easy to catch up with everyone. The purpose of the luncheon we were attending was to remedy that failing.

Held in the church gym, it was a monthly event to which we all brought and shared our food. Philip was seated at my table.

'Jana Woldt,' I returned.

'I'm from England,' Philip said.

'Yeah. I think I knew that,' I grinned. His English accent was so quaint I could hardly make out what he was saying and had to listen intently as he continued.

'Sevenoaks in Kent,' he said. 'And you?'

'Oh, my folks are from a small place you'd never've heard of – about four hours' drive north of New York City. But I left home four years ago and I've been in Richmond for two.'

My mom and dad had lived most of their married life in a modest woodframed house in Poestenkill, New York State, where they'd raised me and my three sisters, Wendy, Amy and Heidi. The younger ones, at only ten and twelve years of age, didn't even seem like sisters to me, but Wendy was only two years my junior. Recently married, she had settled in a place close by my parents.

The flat which I now occupied was in an elegant town house on Linden Row and since my move I'd taken up employment as Charter Sales Manager at Metropolitan Coach Corporation.

'I'm in charge of hiring out coaches to groups and I organise charters and trips,' I said, in reply to Philip's query.

He, I learned, was a scientist, had a B.Sc. with Honours in Medical Biochemistry, had gained a Ph.D. at Birmingham University and now, aged twenty-five, was in his first post-doctorate job at the Department of Pharmacology in the Medical College of Virginia.

He was cute, and I liked his boyish good looks and zany sense of humour. Pretty soon I found myself in his company more and more, laughing at his English terminology – swimming costume, where we'd say bathing suit – exercising at the gym, and generally goofing about and being silly. Phil was mad about movies – horror films mostly – and had been president of the film club at his university. In the company of others from our Sunday School class, we frequented the local cinemas and spent endless hours discussing the merits of what we'd seen. Teasingly, he taught me how to drink tea properly and educated me in the habits and mores of England – from cricket to punk rock! Sometimes he'd cook dinner for me and occasionally he'd hold my hand. Philip Godfrey, I told myself, was one of the most romantic guys I'd ever dated.

By Christmas, 1982, nine months after our first meeting, I knew I was falling in love. I'd often wondered what it would be like and how I would know. Now I knew. I, who had always had a weight problem, began shedding the unwanted pounds spontaneously.

Sometimes, though he never allowed it to curtail any activity, Phil appeared to be in some considerable pain. Dressed in his habitual scruffy jeans and T-shirt, he'd look almost comical as he limped along, a bandage tied roughly round his knee or elbow. However, if asked about the cause, or if anyone showed sympathy, he'd laugh it off and joke about his 'war wound'. Then one day in February, 1983, soon after our first kiss on Valentine's Day and nearly a year after our initial meeting, I learned the truth behind his apparent lightheartedness.

We'd been dining at one of our favourite restaurants, the Robin Inn on Robinson Street, and, seated across the table with its red and white checked cloth, Phil kept his eyes lowered behind his gold-framed glasses.

'I'm a haemophiliac,' he explained, hesitantly, and pulled out his identification card to show me.

I'd never met one before and my knowledge of the subject was nil.

'I realised that I was different when I was really young,' he told me, in response to my prompting. 'I couldn't physically do the things that my friends and sisters could do.'

Phil had shown me photos of his sisters. Paulette, two years younger than he, was a nurse. She had a wide, open face framed with thick, curly brown hair, and a warm expansive smile. Patrina, fair and pretty, looked shyer and quieter and was the youngest of the family. She, so Phil had told me, was training to be a Norland Nanny, as their mother had.

Phil stirred his coffee, whirling the dark liquid round and round, then abruptly halted its flow with the bowl of the spoon. For a moment he stared at the miniature vortex then tapped the spoon against the edge of the cup and laid it in the saucer.

'Even at that point I realised how much I had to rely on my family and friends for things,' he continued. 'When I had bleeds – internally, into joints – I remember being in a lot of pain. Intense pain. And having to take masses of pain-killers. I missed an awful lot of school.'

Phil's voice dropped away. He fiddled with his coffee spoon for a few moments then resumed his story once more.

'There were some sports the school wouldn't allow me to do. Cricket was one. It was considered too dangerous. Mum even volunteered to take responsibility if anything happened to me, but it made no difference. It was so frustrating.'

He frowned and his face took on an expression, which I was fast recognising as typical, of his determination to brook no quarter as far as his disability was concerned. On the table between us, a candle burned. Molten wax had formed a semi-liquid pool at its base and Phil jabbed at the viscid puddle with one finger before he looked up at me again. Clearly, he was finding all this self-revelation rather too much. Wasn't that what they always said about Englishmen? I smiled, encouragingly, and urged him to continue.

'I don't remember much about junior school – probably 'cause I missed so much of it,' he went on. 'My big memory is my car accident when I was eleven. I was coming home from school and I was late. I got off the bus and ran behind it without looking at the traffic on the other side of the road. I'd almost reached the curb, when I realised that I wasn't going to make it. The wing of a car hit my pelvis and I fell and rolled over on the grass verge. The driver jumped out and rushed over to me; but when I said I wasn't seriously injured he took me home. Then my mother took me to the hospital, where I had an X-ray.'

'And?' I prompted.

He shrugged, carelessly. 'There were no broken bones. So I just had a tetanus jab and we went home again.'

For a moment silence fell between us, then Phil looked directly at me. His eyes crinkled.

'The reason I was in a hurry to get home in the first place,' he said, with barely suppressed mirth, 'was that I wanted to watch *Time Tunnel* on TV!'

I laughed. He was incorrigible. TV first. Health and safety last!

'So what happened then?'

'This was Tuesday,' he continued, more soberly. 'By Friday I was so weak and looked so anaemic, we had to call our family doctor. He took me straight to hospital. That's when we realised how serious the bleeding was. I was haemorrhaging internally everywhere. So I had a blood transfusion. And from what I remember, in about two and a half weeks, I had eight pints of blood and fifteen of plasma.'

I gasped, and slopped my coffee in the saucer.

'On the Friday I went in, they tried operating on my hip to suck the blood off. To relieve the pressure of the bruise. It was semi-clotted so that didn't work. I don't remember anything of the weekend.'

'Boy!' I exclaimed. 'That's hardly surprising.'

Phil warmed to his theme. 'On the Monday the doctors started on me in earnest. They found I was bleeding in my chest, which worried them. I was on the danger list for a few days because they were concerned that if it didn't stop, I wouldn't survive. Then towards the end of the week, when the danger was less, they decided to operate on the clot in my hip. They got rid of it.

But it caused terrible haemorrhaging that wouldn't stop. They couldn't sew it up because they were afraid that if they did it would start bleeding again when they took the stitches out. So for about a week I lay in a pool of blood.'

I grimaced. 'What happened?'

'Blood came out as quickly as it went in. But gradually it slowed down. And over a couple of weeks it stopped.' Phil shrugged.

In the silence that followed, I stared at him in admiration. The circumstances he'd described and the pain he'd so evidently endured made his infectious humour all the more remarkable. And heaven alone knew how he'd achieved so much academically!

'It's a miracle you ever got any education with all that time off school,' I said.

Phil grinned, dismissively. 'When I was getting better, the teacher would visit and give me work to do.'

I set down my empty cup on the saucer and pushed it from me. 'But you must have been bored out of your mind being in hospital so long,' I insisted.

'Actually, I had a good time with the other kids in there. Especially with one who had leukaemia. I used to push him around the ward in a chair until the nurses put a stop to it. They thought it a bit dangerous.'

'A bit dangerous?' I exclaimed. 'I should think it was!' I shook my head and grinned. That sort of understatement sounded just like Phil!

'The best thing about my accident,' he concluded, 'was that through it we managed to be put in contact with the Haemophilia Centre. At the Royal Free Hospital in London. I was the first haemophiliac my consultant in Ipswich had known. So he took a special interest in my case.'

'Is there nothing they can do to stop the bleeding?' I asked. 'I mean, could what you've described happen again?'

Phil signalled to the waiter and settled the bill.

'I finally got treatment called Cryo – short for Cryo-precipitate,' he said. 'Later, in the seventies, that was superceded by Factor VIII, which is far more effective. It replaces the blood product that's missing in a haemophiliac. It's vital to have treatment as soon as a bleed starts because otherwise it can have damaging longterm effects on your joints. Also, it keeps the pain and incapacitation to a minimum. In my case – since I have nought per cent clotting factor in my blood – it literally stops me from bleeding to death.'

He rose from the table, helped me to shrug on my coat, took me by the hand and threaded his way between the tables, towards the door. Together we stepped out of the cosily lit interior into the dark street outside.

'I suppose you could say that antihaemophilic globulin – or Factor VIII as it's popularly known – is my lifesaver,' he said in conclusion as we walked off into the night.

Life saver? A wolf in sheep's clothing might more accurately have described what was to follow, had we but known. But this was 1983. And at that stage the contamination of Factor VIII with the AIDS virus, was little more than a rumour in a research scientist's test tube.

* * *

In many respects, the attraction between Phil and me was one of opposites. He embraced life with an enthusiasm that was over and beyond my more conservative outlook, and he introduced me to a whole new perspective in entertainment, from Demolition Derbies – where old cars were raced until immobilised – to reggae concerts and football matches. With his mania for movies, he would think nothing of searching out late-night 'flea-pits' in order to widen his choice of viewing and, with the eagerness of a buff, 'educated' me in the art of horror and its special effects.

Yet for all that, there were aspects of American life that he didn't hesitate to criticise. And with the passing of time, I began to worry that he failed to see me as a person in my own right and saw only someone tainted by this prejudice.

Despite these differences, however, by April I knew that I wanted to marry Phil. There had been times when I'd almost despaired of ever meeting anyone with whom I could share my life and I'd even wondered if God *really* cared. However, having found Phil for me, and allowed me to fall in love with him, the question now was: had the Lord imbued Phil with similar feelings for me?

Adolescent fears returned to haunt me.

'I'm the pretty one and you're the brainy one,' my sister, Wendy, was wont to say, deprecatingly, throughout our teenage years and, looking at my ordinary features, spectacles, and unremarkable brown hair, I'd had no option but to agree.

Mature reason prevailed, however. Perhaps some of the men I'd dated in the past *had* felt threatened by the extent of my education but I was certain that this could not be so with Phil. My degree in Linguistics could hardly be seen as competitive in the light of his brilliant academic achievements.

I began to wonder whether or not to take the risk of telling Phil how I felt. I didn't want to scare him off but I knew that if he returned to England in March '84 – when his post-doctorate position in the USA came to an end – there would be an end, too, to our relationship. Earnestly, I began to pray, together with my prayer partner, for a more satisfactory conclusion. Towards the close of summer, I could contain myself no longer.

'Have you ever thought of marriage, Phil?' I asked him.

'Some day, perhaps,' he said, vaguely.

I shared my anxieties with my mom.

'Well, he must like you, Jan,' she said when I told her of our romance.

'Yeah . . . ' I agreed doubtfully. 'But I'm twenty-eight, Mom. Time is not on my side.'

Finally, it seemed that events might come to a head. When Phil expressed a desire to go to the Caribbean, it was natural – since I worked in the travel industry – that I should investigate the possibilities; and more natural yet that, after poring over brochures for hours, we should decide to go together. Accordingly, I made the necessary reservations and opened a joint savings account. And as the date of our departure drew closer, we talked more and more about marriage.

'If you asked me,' I told him, 'I'd definitely say yes.'

'I'm not sure I know what Being In Love is,' said Phil.

I made up my mind that if he didn't ask me to marry him soon then our relationship would have to finish with our holiday. I'd just have to get over him somehow.

During a two-day stop-over in New York we took in Phil's favourite movie *Little Shop of Horrors* off Broadway, then completed our journey, to arrive in Barbados on Monday 14th November. Swimming, snorkelling, cruising, discoing and driving round the West Indian island in a Minimoke – it was an idyllic holiday, spoiled only by the absence of my yearned-for proposal.

After several missed opportunities, I was in the depths of despair. We'd reached our last evening together and Phil had made no move. With a heavy heart I dressed carefully for dinner and together we went off to dine at the Pisces Restaurant. A waiter showed us to a table by the water's edge where palm trees dipped and danced in the breeze and the whisper of waves caressed the shore.

Surely, now, I thought.

Diffidently at first, but gaining courage with each course of our meal, Phil began to unfold a story. A story of – not his undying love for me – but the entire plot of Tolkein's *The Lord Of The Rings* – his favourite book!

I should have known that he was nervous, but I was too nervous myself! Finally, when the meal had been cleared, he said: 'Well, she's drinking her coffee and wondering if he's going to ask her to marry him. And the answer is . . . ?'

With dignity, I replied. 'I'll wait till I'm properly asked.'
'Will you marry me?' Phil promptly responded.

*   *   *

Later, wandering hand in hand along the moonlit beach –
the most romantic moment of my life – I was overcome
with nervous excitement. Suddenly, my stomach parted
company with my dinner.

'Tell me when it's over,' Phil said with revulsion and
covering his ears, he turned away.

From then on the romance gave way to 'sick jokes'.

*   *   *

Phil and I were married on the evening of 24th March,
1984 at First Baptist Church, Richmond, Virginia. I wore
the white taffeta gown I had made myself, whilst Phil, in
a grey morning suit, looked very stylish for once. We'd
written our own vows so that they were personal to us
alone and it was with great solemnity that we committed
ourselves to one another:

> I thank God for bringing us together. I look forward
> to sharing my life with you. I pray that my heart will
> always be open to you and yours to mine. I love you
> as a friend and equal. I will not try to change you, for
> I accept you as you are. I will be honest, faithful, and
> will work with you through good times and bad, so that
> our marriage can mean for ever.

For ever! Together. How naïvely I spoke the words. Only
in hindsight was I to come anywhere near understanding the true meaning of the concept of togetherness in
eternity.

With the formal part over, however, and the wedding
guests assembled for photographs, we agreed, with a great
deal of hilarity, that a change of name from Woldt to

Godfrey was no retrograde step. Three weeks later, after a brief honeymoon in Colonial Williamsburg, we took the evening flight to England. A return for Phil. A one-way ticket for me.

On 1st May, a fortnight later, Phil began a new job with the Medical Research Council Unit and University Department of Clinical Pharmacology, Oxford. On the strength of his salary – which was negligible, to my mind – we were able to purchase a tiny terraced house in Percy Street, and thought ourselves fortunate to have been offered, along with our low-start mortgage, a three-year life assurance as part of the package.

Approached via a wrought-iron gate and a short path from the pavement, number seventy-three was a Victorian two-up two-down with a pocket-handkerchief-sized garden at the back, which Phil and his dad dug and put down to lawn. Inside, a russet carpet, red sofa-bed from Habitat and bookshelves completed the warm and friendly atmosphere that we were at pains to create. The Godfrey household was established.

By Christmas, we had settled happily enough to married life and only Phil's occasional bleeds marred our contented existence. Until, that was, the evening of 17th September, 1985.

* * *

It had been a grey day, with a lowering sky that had clung tenaciously to the earth's contours, shrouding the spires of Christ Church Cathedral in unseasonally heavy, swirling mist. Seventy-three Percy Street afforded little protection against the permeating damp and, despite drawn curtains and the gasfire which I'd lit in the sitting-room on my return from work, there was no warmth to be found. Certainly none that reached the tiny kitchen at the back of the house.

On one side of the narrow room, at the far end of the Formica worktop, an array of food and utensils awaited attention. On a plate lay two fillets of plaice, as yet bereft of a coating of the seasoned flour I had mixed earlier that evening. Beneath the single light bulb that hung from the kitchen ceiling, they looked naked and exposed. Phil was peeling potatoes under running water at the kitchen sink. Soon, I hoped, he would begin the cooking.

He had elected to make supper – his favourite fish and chips – in order that I could finish the ironing before going on to Bible study. He was good like that, though with less interest in food than I, I sometimes found him infuriatingly slow. My mouth watered.

With the usual topics of conversation exhausted, we'd lapsed into silence. Then without turning from his tasks, Phil began to speak.

'I popped in to the Haemophilia Centre on the way home from work.'

The Centre was a single-storey building set in the grounds of the Churchill Hospital, Headington, and existed for the benefit of those with bleeding disorders. Under the directorship of Dr Charles Rizza, Consultant Physician, some eighteen members of staff were permanently on hand to care for patients and their families, and to advise on all medical and social aspects of haematology, including dental treatment, general health, education, employment, genetic counselling and other areas of personal difficulty.

There was nothing unusual about Phil paying a visit to the Centre. During the eighteen months of our marriage, I'd discovered that a close relationship exists between a haemophiliac and his doctors. Phil went frequently to pick up supplies of Factor VIII concentrate which, in recent years, had become available for home use. I was puzzled, therefore, as to the significance of his visit – but not for long.

'I had an AIDS test.'

Phil blurted out the news as if afraid of my reaction. He kept his back to me, turned off the tap and began cutting the potatoes into chips.

'Oh? What for?'

Behind him, the tap began to drip.

'Didn't you hear the news earlier this week?'

I said nothing.

'The World Health Organisation says AIDS has reached epidemic proportions.'

He lit the gas under the chip pan then turned to look at me. Still I remained silent.

'Sorry, Jana. They'll need to test you too.'

Briskly, I tackled the ironing pile, deftly arranging one of my shirts on the board and jiggling the iron back and forth across the collar, yoke and sleeves.

'Me? Why on earth should they want to test me?' Steam belched from the sole-plate, and at the sink the dripping tap began a slow steady dribble that pinged loudly off a pan lid in the sink.

'It's normal procedure.'

'Normal? Why?'

'Well . . . I suppose there isn't really a normal procedure,' Phil admitted. 'They've only just started doing HIV tests on haemophiliacs . . . But because of the nature of the disease, spouses are at risk too.'

I considered this piece of information. As a scientist, of course, Phil would be well up on such things, whereas I, if I were honest, had no desire to know. With more care than the task warranted, I spread my shirt on the airer.

'Do I really have to have a test?' I asked. 'We're both fit and well. Surely they don't seriously think . . . '

Slowly, Phil tipped the chips into the hot fat. Bubbling and foaming, they surged in the pan. He adjusted the gas, then turned towards me.

'Jana.' Visibly, he steeled himself. 'There's no getting round it. The results of my test are through.'

I banged the iron down hard and made a ferocious attack on a sheet. On the far side of the kitchen, the dripping water gathered momentum, clattering louder and louder on the metal lid, until the sound filled my head. Gushed and pounded in my ears.

Phil turned the tap off, leaned heavily over the sinktop and gripped it on either side. Then swiftly, shoving his hands into his pockets, he swivelled round to the window and stared out into the black night.

'I'm sorry, Boss,' he said, miserably, 'there's no other way of putting it. I'm HIV positive.'

2

The Serpent in the Garden

'You have blessed the work of his hands . . .
But stretch out your hand and strike his flesh
and bones, and he will surely curse you to
your face.'

Job 1:10 and 2:5

We'd called each other Boss as a term of affection ever since we'd seen the movie *My Favourite Year*. It was the story of how television got off the ground in the fifties, and depicted a comedy Gangster Show with a character called 'Boss Hijack'. I could see him still, a big man with well-oiled hair, wearing a pin-stripe suit – quite unlike either Phil or me, but the name had stuck. Somehow, at that moment, the fiction was of more substance to my mind than the stark reality of Phil's news.

I stared across the kitchen. On the stove the frying pan gave off a faint blue smoke that shimmied, unsteadily, in a downdraft from the open window. Outside, tracing an erratic path against the night sky, droplets wrung from the damp air slid and jerked down the glass. Grimly, I tightened my grasp on the iron.

'Frankly,' Phil was saying, 'I wasn't that surprised. About having the HIV antibodies, I mean.'

My heart pounded. If Phil had the antibodies then he was okay, I thought. I'd read little enough about AIDS but

I was pretty sure that this would mean he was protected against getting the full-blown disease.

'I've been following the medical literature since about 1983,' he continued, 'so I knew the virus was transferred by blood and would be a risk for haemophiliacs . . . '

I stared at the back of his head. My best friend at university had said much the same thing when she'd heard that I was planning to marry Phil.

'Aren't you worried about the risk of AIDS?' she'd asked.

'Nope,' I'd blithely replied.

Had I been naïve, expecting God to protect us just because we were Christians? Or had I simply buried my head in the sand?

Phil floured the fish and lowered it into the smoking fat.

'Even so,' he said, wiping his hands on the dishcloth, 'having it confirmed makes me feel as if I've had a death sentence placed over me.' His voice quavered. 'I feel desperately sorry for all the teenagers and kids who had no idea. It must be awful. Suddenly, without warning, having your life ripped out from under you.'

No! No! I didn't want to hear that.

'What does HIV stand for?' I asked, distractedly.

'Human Immunodeficiency Virus,' Phil replied, and turned to look at me. 'I can show you some medical pamphlets, if you'd like to know more . . . ?'

'Oh, drat!' The expletive was torn from my lips. 'Burned myself,' I explained, sucking my finger and blinking hard to disperse the tears that sprang to my eyes. Then I turned away to empty the water from the iron.

Later that night, in the darkness of our bedroom, Phil raised the subject again.

'I was a bit nervous about telling you,' he admitted from the other side of the bed. 'I wasn't sure how you'd take it.'

I lay with my back to him, clinging to the edge of the mattress, and stared, until my eyes hurt, at the broad strip of harsh orange light that infiltrated the curtains from the street lamp outside.

'Did you . . . Did you . . . suspect?' Phil persevered.

I moved further from the warmth of his body, unable to bring myself to curl up close, as usual.

'No,' I said, shortly.

For a few moments we lay isolated with our own thoughts. Then reluctantly I asked the question that was uppermost in my mind.

'What will happen, Phil?'

The deathly hush that followed said it all. Then Phil cleared his throat.

'I . . . I don't know . . . '

A tear slid, unseen, down my cheek. Far away, muffled by the blanketing fog, a motorcycle roared through the dark, and downstairs, the front room clock chimed twelve. As the hours of night flowed turgidly downhill to morning, Phil's inert body told me, gradually, that he slept.

The silence was profound; obscure and alienating. Like the mist that eddied against the windowpane.

*   *   *

For a week or so, I could not bring myself to touch or be touched. Yet it was not Phil whom I wordlessly reviled. I was filled with revulsion and felt as if all physical contact between us had been debased – soiled by a faceless, nameless stranger that had invaded the body of the one I loved. Sensitive to my distress, Phil made no further attempts to enlighten me on a subject which had, so shockingly and threateningly, thrust itself upon us.

Strangely, it did not occur to me to apportion blame: either to God or to mankind. Nor was anger a problem. There was nothing ultra-spiritual in my quiet acquiescence, however. As far as I was concerned neither blame nor anger served any useful purpose; and in any case, I was too busy coping with the daily bombardment of AIDS news.

Suddenly, everywhere I turned, I was confronted with

media-mania. AIDS was news. Big news. Articles abounded. TV programmes proliferated. Radio waves reverberated. The issues were given global coverage. I was sure that not even the Black Death of medieval times could have made so great an impact on humanity, as this modern scourge of the eighties.

I hated the word AIDS. To my ears it sounded horrid and ugly. Certainly, it was not a word I could apply to Phil. HIV positive was more acceptable. HIV antibodies more acceptable still.

There was hope in that term, or so it seemed to me. With little understanding of the infection, and no desire for greater comprehension, I could happily delude myself. Antibodies were nature's defence system – that much I knew. Furthermore, they could be induced – as in the case of vaccination (or was it immunisation, I was never sure?) – in order to combat infection. Thus, I reasoned.

And anything that threatened that line of reason was anathema to me. I refused to read anything on the matter. If a news item on the virus, or the story of a victim was shown on TV whilst I was watching, I would instantly leave the room. If that proved impracticable, I'd switch channels. And if that failed, and for some reason I was caught with no option but to listen, a sense of helplessness would wash over me and I would dissolve into tears.

One evening I sat down to watch one of our favourite TV shows, *St Elsewhere*. The storyline was of a group of doctors working in a rundown hospital. It was good entertainment with realistic and identifiable situations which usually had the power to lift me out of myself. On this occasion, however, faced with one of the characters who had been infected with AIDS, the situation was all too realistic and identifiable. I sobbed, uncontrollably.

Phil, by contrast, seemed to cope so much better than I. No one knew of his infection. Yet if we met with prejudice of any sort, without fail he would gently attempt to help me see reason.

'Don't be hard on them, Boss. It's only ignorance and fear that makes them talk like that. They don't know what they're saying.'

Though frequently short on patience with himself, and with the limitations imposed upon his body when he had bleeds, Phil unerringly 'saw the other side'. I had always admired this attribute in him, especially as I felt so impatient, myself, when confronted with people who didn't act as I thought they should. By my own observation, it was clear that Phil had a faith which was finely woven into the warp and weft of his being: the fabric of his very life.

Although I had grown up in a Christian home and had attended church regularly, beside Phil's example my faith seemed superficial. Up to the time we had met, I'd always thought of people as being basically good and this, perhaps, explained my disappointment when they failed to live up to my expectations. Through Phil, however, I had discovered that there isn't a single person who is 'good' when measured beside the infinite goodness of God. That concept constitutes one of the basic tenets of the Christian creed and suddenly, I'd realised, that in subscribing to a belief in man's underlying goodness, I'd unwittingly negated the need for Jesus' death.

That thinking, clearly, was in error. Jesus had died for *sinners*. However, though I'd believed in Him for my salvation and knew that He'd paid the price for my sin and restored my relationship with God, that relationship had been lacking in depth on a day-to-day basis. It was rather like an arranged marriage with someone I'd never met.

Since meeting Phil that had changed. Gradually through church attendance, Bible study and prayer, my understanding and love of God had become deeper and stronger. Together, we'd grown, and day by day, our trust in the

Lord was expanding. In the words of the Bible, perseverance was developing our faith.

Just how, and to what extent that faith would be tested, I, for one, couldn't even begin to hazard a guess.

*   *   *

Gradually, normality returned to our relationship. In fact, in a short time, *so* normal was our life together, that we continued to conduct our sexual activity as before – without protection. Frankly, with no evidence of disease, it simply did not occur to either of us to do otherwise; it was easier to accept the *status quo*. A change of behaviour in this respect would have necessitated action on our part: the purchase and use of condoms. In any case, that particular mode of protection was abhorrent to us both and would have seemed obtrusive and mechanical.

After a while, however, Phil evidently had second thoughts and began to use a sheath – though only just before ejaculation.

'It takes away all spontaneity and sensation . . . ' I complained.

Miserably, Phil agreed. 'I find it depressing too,' he admitted. 'Having to think about safe sex certainly puts a damper on how much passion I can put into our relationship. It seems terrible that the very thing that used to give us so much pleasure should suddenly have become so dangerous.'

'It's no more dangerous than it was yesterday or last week,' I reasoned.

'But I didn't realise the consequences then . . . '

'I'm prepared to take the risk . . . '

'Well, I'm not! Being HIV positive brings a whole new set of attitudes to bear on our love life. We *must* make changes – and that means taking precautions.'

'Oh, Phil! Do we have to?' I said, with bad grace.

'Yes!' he replied, firmly. 'It's a huge worry to me to think that when I want to give you joy I might also be giving you pain and illness. I feel as if I'm playing Russian roulette – gambling with your health like that.'

For some time we continued in this vein until, prompted by staff at the Haemophilia Centre, I was asked to accompany Phil on one of his regular appointments to see Dr Rizza.

Charles Rizza had attended Phil during the year and a half since our arrival in Oxford. He must have been about five foot eight or nine, I guessed, a stocky man with grey hair that formed wings at the sides, and a clipped, goatee-type beard. His age I judged to be fifty-plus. Of Scottish and Italian extraction, he spoke with a slight lilt – and he immediately put me at ease. Clearly, he was both sensitive and sympathetic to our plight.

First, I learned that, prior to 1955, treatment of haemophiliacs had been purely diagnostic, and that with no known medication, they had had to suffer the most appalling pain and crippling damage to joints and muscles that were swollen from internal bleeding. The state of Phil's limbs bore testimony to those early days. Attempts had been made to arrest external bleeds by the use of blood transfusions but, not surprisingly, fifty per cent of all patients had died before the age of forty.

Eventual research and development had led to the extraction of the clotting agent Factors VIII and IX from samples of whole blood. And whilst cross-infection of diseases like hepatitis sometimes occurred, this had been a relatively minor problem, in that it was usually confined to a particular batch. Later, however, when production had been taken up by various manufacturers for commercial enterprise, the pooling of blood from numerous sources could result in huge quantities being contaminated by just one donor.

'Homosexual donors at least had the same altruistic aims as heterosexuals,' said Dr Rizza. 'Whereas alcoholics and drug addicts were in it purely for gain – to feed their habit. When it became known that American blood –

which we used here in Britain – was being donated by down-and-outs, the British Government stated that the UK had to become self-sufficient.'

Phil, it seemed, had almost certainly been infected by American products, though when and where was not clear. Irrational though it might be, I couldn't help feeling that it was a sobering and shameful slur on my fellow countrymen. To think that they should have inflicted so terrible a disease on any human being, let alone one who had already suffered so much pain.

'Despite all that,' Phil said, 'even had I known the risks of HIV, I'd still have chosen to have Factor VIII. It improved my quality of life beyond measure.'

Dr Rizza nodded agreement, then moved on to the comparatively more sensitive issues of intimacy.

'You do need to take proper precautions,' he advised, leaning back on his chair and hooking an arm over the back. 'The AIDS virus is passed on in semen as well as blood and blood products. Unprotected sexual intercourse would put Jana at risk, and though, frankly, we don't yet know enough about how the disease is transmitted, I'd advise the use of a condom at all times during penetration.'

We left feeling somewhat depressed.

Later, Mary Fletcher, our social worker at the Centre, told me that the staff found dealing with the sexual behaviour of their patients – most of whom they'd known for many years – a new and delicate area of discussion. 'It's embarrassing suddenly having to intrude upon the private lives of people whom you otherwise know well,' she said, 'especially when that involves counselling couples together.'

I had to admit that I found some of the questions we were posed unnecessary, irrelevant and uncomfortable. However, when it was pointed out to me that maximum information from all sources would result in a more comprehensive picture for research, I complied – if not eagerly, then at least willingly enough.

The same could not be said when it came to putting Dr Rizza's advice into practice. In order to regulate my periods, I wanted to go on taking the pill. It seemed silly, having to use two methods of contraception but, reluctantly, I agreed that there was nothing we could do about it. And eventually we became accustomed to the mechanics of using a sheath – though we liked them not at all.

*   *   *

Breaking the news to our parents was something we liked still less. Phil's mum and dad were due to visit us one day in November and we both agreed that it would be kinder to tell them face to face than by telephone or letter. As the time for their visit approached, we steeled ourselves for the ordeal.

Peter Godfrey was one of the directors at Chem Systems in St James's Square, London. As a consultant for the chemical industry, he travelled abroad on business quite frequently: Japan, South America, USA, Africa and Europe. Tall, with a military bearing and receding hairline, he nevertheless had a kind and approachable demeanour and, as an Elder of Vine Evangelical Church, was well used to counselling those who were suffering.

Phil's mum, Pat Godfrey, was a tall, elegant lady with beautifully coiffed grey hair. During the eighteen months of my marriage to Phil, I'd come to know and like her enormously and she left me in no doubt that the feeling was mutual.

'You're not really like an American, Jana,' she would say, meaning it as a compliment. 'You're not loud like some of those we met during our stay in the States.'

'Mum means you're not brash,' Dad had added, by way of explanation.

Sociable and gracious, Mum had a way of instantly putting people at their ease.

'You poor things,' she said, when Phil had haltingly

related the details of his AIDS test. Concern filled her face and she reached out to cover my hand with her own, saying, 'What happens now?'

Phil shrugged. 'I don't know . . . '

'But you've seen Dr Rizza?' she asked, looking from one to the other of us. 'Didn't he give you any indication?'

Phil didn't answer.

'We don't know much at all, at the moment,' I admitted. 'It was all rather a shock . . . '

'Yes,' Mrs Godfrey paused. 'And yet . . . I suppose we half expected something like this, didn't we, Peter?' She looked at her husband for confirmation.

Dad took out a clean white handkerchief and blew his nose hard. 'It's difficult to know what the Lord has in mind,' he said, sinking down next to Phil on our red Habitat settee, 'but He's watched over you all this time, son. He won't stop now.'

Beside Dad's bulk, Phil looked slight, even thin; but then he'd never had much of an appetite.

'We've all had to live with this for a long time,' Mum agreed and, as if shelving the problems of the future until such times as our minds could grapple with them, she turned to the past – to what had already been successfully surmounted. 'It was a complete surprise when the doctors discovered that Phil was a haemophiliac,' she explained to me. 'There was no history of it in the family.'

Dad turned to Phil. 'I remember when we found out. It was Whitsun. You were only a little chap and I felt awful that there was nothing I could do to change things – to cure you.' His eyes darkened with pain as he recalled.

'Two and a quarter, he was,' Mum said. 'He fell down just outside the gate of our house and cut his gum. After a while it stopped bleeding and I forgot about it. The following day he did exactly the same thing again but this time it wouldn't stop bleeding and there he was – lying in a pool of blood.'

'We had to get the doctor to come . . . ' Dad interjected.

'And all he could say was that he thought Phil was aggravating the sore by sucking his thumb,' Mum went on. 'We had to spend all night watching him – to keep his thumb out of his mouth. But it still wouldn't stop bleeding. When the doctor called next day, he said Phil would have to go into hospital in Margate for observation.'

'It was quite a distance. We were living in Ramsgate . . . ' said Dad.

'And that's when they found the haemophilia?' I asked.

Mum nodded. 'But not until after they'd ruled out leukaemia.'

'Then there was the bump on his head . . . ' said Dad.

Mum laughed, shortly. ' . . . And the bruise in his groin. And the time he lost his tooth . . . '

I looked at her with admiration. 'It must have been a dreadful worry for you,' I said. 'Phil was obviously an active child . . . Weren't you terrified to let him out of your sight?'

Phil struggled to his feet. He always stiffened up when he'd been sitting for any length of time.

'They never made a big deal of it,' he said, going over to the stereo and putting on a Jimmy Cliff record, 'The Harder They Come'. 'If I had a really bad bleed – about once a month – one of them would drive me to London to the Royal Free. Or I'd go by ambulance. I'd have an injection of Cryo and then we'd come home. But they never stopped me doing anything within reason. And when I couldn't walk, Mum would bring me to school on a scooter rather than let me miss out.'

Mum nodded. 'Yes . . . Thinking about it, I suppose we were quite tough with you. I remember when we moved to Ipswich in December 'sixty-four . . . It was a bitterly cold winter but you still went off to play every day on the Heath with Paulette.' She turned to me. 'But then life wouldn't have been much fun for him if he'd been wrapped in cotton wool, would it?'

'I'm glad,' Phil said, seating himself. 'That sort of attitude made the other kids treat me normally. I remember one friend from church – Mark Smith – he'd adapt our playing according to whether I could walk or not. If I could only hop, then we'd play hopping games.'

He paused, pushing up the sleeves of his shirt to the elbow, in a familiar habit. He hated to have his forearms covered, though he never exposed his joints, saying that they were too ugly and swollen to be revealed.

'A lot of the time I was able to forget I had haemophilia and just get on with life . . . ' Phil continued. 'Though I suppose it took me a long time to learn how much I could physically do without getting a bleed.'

Mum smiled. 'You were always game to try anything . . . '

Dad turned to me. 'Philip always wanted to get to the top of the mountain,' he said, 'both physically and metaphorically speaking! Everything was a challenge to him. He was never content just to mess around on the nursery slopes, so to speak. His one aim was to scale the heights.'

'He hurried into the world when he was born,' said Mum, 'and he's never stopped hurrying since . . . '

As if suddenly aware that this latest development might be the one thing that stopped Phil dead in his tracks, we all lapsed into silence.

Dad was the first to break into our thoughts. 'I remember we had the church elders round to pray for healing for you, when we first found out you had haemophilia,' he said, looking at Phil.

'We were members of the Brethren Church in Ramsgate in those days,' Mum explained to me. 'We were dreadfully disappointed when Phil had his next bleed and it was obvious that he hadn't been healed.'

Dad sighed. 'Haemophilia was totally unknown territory to us,' he agreed. 'But the point is, that we also prayed for the strength to cope with the problem – for Philip and for ourselves – and that's what I think we should do now. If you'd like us to?'

Phil's eyes met mine and we nodded.

'It seems to me,' Dad said, 'that we should pray for

Phil to continue to be in good health – as he is now.
And for God's blessing on you both,' he continued, as
he laid hands on each of our shoulders. 'You'll need all
the guidance, wisdom and faith that the Lord can bestow
upon you. There are bound to be trials ahead.'

Mum stood at his side and together they prayed.

Peace flooded into my heart. And with the Lord's hand
upon us, the trials were kept at bay. At least for the
time being.

* * *

Even when both sets of parents had been acquainted
with the facts of Phil's infection, we still said nothing
to anyone else – with the exception of my American
university friend, Ruth. Dr Rizza's advice had extended
still further: that in response to enquiry, we should avoid
the truth. No one could be sure of the reaction we would
receive and besides, my philosophy was that the less we
spoke of the subject, the easier it would be to continue
a normal life. Phil, I suspected, kept himself informed of
the latest developments; but for my part, I just wanted
to forget.

And to a large extent, I succeeded. Within a year of
Phil's diagnosis, I had plans for the future. Determined to
start a family, and cocooned with the bliss of ignorance, I
set about persuading Phil.

'Honey,' I began, 'it's natural for a woman to want a
baby. I don't want to be denied that opportunity.'

We were curled up in bed together, our duvet a warm
and secure nest, despite the summer season. The overhead
light was on as we hadn't – as yet – been through the
ritual good-natured argument about who was to get up
to turn it off at the door. Lying in the crook of Phil's
arm, with my head on his shoulder, I traced circles
with my finger, smoothing the light covering of hair on
his chest.

'It would be far too risky . . . ' he countered.

'No, it wouldn't. Lots of the other wives are pregnant. Linda told me.'

Linda Jones was the other social worker assigned to Phil and me at the Haemophilia Centre. Tall and slender, her oval face framed with short brown hair, she was someone in whom I'd found sympathy and understanding. She was a good listener and despite her unmarried status, she'd instantly seemed to appreciate my desire for motherhood.

'If you mean the wives of other haemophiliacs,' Phil said, tucking his chin close to his chest so that he could peer down at me, 'they were either pregnant before they knew of the risks, or they had AI.'

I sighed. Artificial Insemination had been presented to me as a solution to the problem, in order to eliminate the risk of conceiving a baby contaminated with the AIDS virus. However, as far as I was concerned, it was not an option.

'I know that, Boss,' I said. 'But that's not the point. It's *your* baby I want, not some nameless, faceless stranger's. I want our baby to come into being as the result of a loving union between us . . . You just don't understand. It wouldn't be the same . . . '

'I am trying to understand, dear. But how do you think I'd feel if you or the baby were infected?'

'Linda's been keeping me informed about the risk levels,' I said, swiftly. 'It's much less before the onset of the first illness. Almost minimal, I should think. I'm not worried . . . '

'But even if all went well – if you conceived without being infected, even if the baby was born okay – there would still be problems. What if anything happens to me? How could I take care of you both?'

I moved away from him so that I could see him better. Without his glasses, he looked even younger and more vulnerable than I'd ever known him. Clearly, he was worried.

'Nothing's gonna happen to you, Boss,' I reassured him.

'And besides, you have life assurance. And then there's the house . . . '

'But that's just the point, Jana. The life assurance attached to the low-cost endowment we took out was only for three years. All the latest info points to the fact that insurance companies are refusing to give cover for anyone who's HIV positive . . . '

'But that's only at home in the States – in the gay community. And in any case . . . '

'I'm telling you, Boss, when our term is up next spring, we could have real problems with insurance . . . '

I propped myself up on one elbow and stroked his face with a strand of my hair.

'But honey, nothin's gonna happen,' I said, again, looking deep into his eyes. 'The Lord'll look after us . . . '

* * *

And so He did. Eventually, with Phil's blessing, I came off the pill and throughout the next few months, God was with us, protecting me from infection and blessing our union. In no time I'd conceived. By November, 1986, after a holiday in Greece together, I was thrilled to be able tell Phil that I was three months pregnant.

He promptly went down with shingles.

We didn't relate Phil's illness to his condition in any way. He'd had ordinary colds from the time he'd been diagnosed HIV positive, but we'd put that down to normal twentieth-century life. Shingles, we thought, was no different; after all, other family members had had it too.

In a short time, Phil was up and about his normal business once more, and off to work in his jeans and favourite red and white striped hand-knitted jumper, now hopelessly threadbare and misshapen from age. For a time, life went on as normal in the Percy Street household.

Then, one day, we learned that Phil's fears regarding
house insurance were well founded. As the expiry date
drew nearer, we were informed that we would be required
to renew the policy ourselves. Already most application
forms posed the question 'Have you ever been tested for
HIV' and in the light of almost certain discrimination, we
decided that there was little point in our applying. Our
trust would have to be in God alone.

*   *   *

I'd worked with Selfridges in Oxford since the Christmas
after our arrival, when a part-time seasonal post had been
offered me on a permanent basis. Within a few weeks, I'd
then been offered advancement and, after taking a short
course for supervisors, was put on a team helping to train
the store's sales staff in the use of a new system of Point
Of Sale – cash tills to the uninitiated. From there, I'd
progressed to the fashion floor's Lingerie Department,
where I was trained to measure and fit clients for bras,
girdles and other foundation garments and thence to
an assistant managerial post in the Haby and Fabrics
Department.

With sewing and craft my hobby, this had suited me
down to the ground, but as my pregnancy began to draw
to an end, I found that I was greatly looking forward to
being a full-time housewife. True, we would feel the pinch
financially. That, however, I was sure would be more than
compensated for by the extra time and effort I would be
able to put into homemaking. My practical skills could
be better employed in our tiny terraced home. And then
there was the baby's layette.

'And how's "Little Ulf" today?' Phil would ask fondly,
setting aside my needlework to run his hand over my
swollen abdomen.

With the typical zeal of a cineaste, he'd nicknamed our
baby after someone we'd seen in the credits of a film –
Gorky Park.

'She's doing fine,' I announced with dignity, hopeful that our baby would be a girl. With three sisters in my family, I had to confess to a marked ignorance in the ways of little boys.

'"Ulfette,"' Phil countered, to accommodate my genetic preferences. 'My little "Ulfette".'

Finally one evening, my waters broke and Phil took me into hospital. After some difficulty overnight, a scan revealed that the baby was in a breach position and we were informed that a Caesarean section would be necessary. On 12th May, 1987, to my great joy, and Phil's too, I was delivered of a baby girl – very blue, but very beautiful.

'Natasha Jana,' Phil announced, when I came round in recovery. They were the names he, himself, had chosen for his small daughter.

However, though the proudest and fondest of fathers, he reserved the right, when we returned home a week later, to endow her with a variety of nicknames: Squidoms, Diddy Pardner and Tiddler, to name but a few. Watching the two of them together, I felt that my cup would surely run over.

*   *   *

By the end of the month, a tiresome cough that had been troubling Phil for some weeks worsened considerably and it became obvious that he was far from well. To begin with, we both put his general feelings of malaise down to tiredness – overwork and sleepless nights with the baby. He had been putting in a lot of overtime at the lab, as he had two students who were starting a project under his direction and, in addition, had had to prepare for a one-day scientific meeting in London. A forthcoming international meeting in Sydney, Australia, had also required his attention as he sought funding to enable him to attend. Soon, however, there was no disguising the fact that Phil's condition was more serious than we had at first supposed.

'I feel so ill,' he said, his body racked with persistent bouts of coughing.

One day, he returned early from work, in a worse state than ever, his face a sickly pallor beneath a sheen of sweat. Stumbling into the front room, he came across me feeding Natasha.

'I feel breathless all the time,' he admitted, when I tackled him. 'Could hardly even make it up the stairs to the lab this morning. Kept feeling I'd have to sit down to get my breath back.'

I looked at him with concern as he sank down on to the settee, his legs flopping over the end, in his favourite – and most comfortable – position.

'Don't you think you ought to see the doctor?' I asked, readjusting Natasha at my breast.

Phil coughed, engulfed in a battle for breath that, for some moments, left him unable to speak. I frowned. It was no good fussing him; he hated to be made to feel an invalid.

'Mike Hardman saw me struggling up the stairs this morning,' he gasped, eventually, naming a colleague at work. 'Of course, being a medic, he insisted on taking me off for an X-ray.'

'And was it okay?' I asked, anxiously.

Phil shrugged, thumping his chest in an effort to clear his lungs. 'Don't know,' he said. 'Must have been something there, I suppose. He suggested I go to the hospital tomorrow and check things over.'

I put the baby over my shoulder to burp her and listened as Phil told me that he had duly made an appointment for the following day, Tuesday, 9th June.

*   *   *

Next morning, we made an early start, setting off for the Churchill Hospital the moment I'd dressed and fed the baby. Once we'd checked in, Phil was shown to a bed on a general ward, and as soon as I had unpacked his bag and stowed his things in the adjacent locker, he was wheeled away for preliminary tests.

I'd come prepared for a lengthy stay but the staff were not too keen on having a baby on the ward, in case she picked up some infection. They showed me to the nurses' room, and when I was settled, I took out my knitting from the baby's changing bag, and began a test square for a sailor's dress I'd planned for Natasha. She slept peacefully in her Moses basket at my feet. Later, when Phil was returned to his bed, we learned that he had pneumocystis and that he would probably be in hospital for a week.

The ward was full of cancer patients, mostly old men, coughing and smoking. The sickly sweet scent of disease hung in the air, mingling with other unidentifiable odours to form a pungent and heady cocktail. I had a headache coming on, and aware that we could have no privacy here, I was glad when it was suggested that Phil be moved into a room of his own that night. At least he'd have a better chance of getting some sleep.

I arrived next day, to find that Phil had had a bronchoscopy and that the diagnosis of pneumocystis was confirmed.

'It's a disease of the lungs – a sort of pneumonia,' Sister reluctantly informed me when I enquired. 'Doctor will see you later to answer your questions.'

Phil was immediately put on medication, delivered intravenously, which made him extremely nauseous. When his boss, Professor David Graham-Smith, visited later in the day, to his great shame, Phil threw up at his feet.

In the meantime, Dr Hopkin took me aside for a chat. He was young and good looking, with a square face, reddish brown hair and a ruddy complexion that made him look a picture of health. He shook my hand, folded his arms across his chest and leaned against the wall.

'I'm afraid the prognosis is not good,' he said with businesslike candour. 'Your husband's condition is very serious.'

'But I thought he . . . The nurse said Phil was responding well to the drugs . . . ' I protested.

Dr Hopkin nodded and said, emphatically, 'That's true. He is making a positive response. However, you have to understand that the nature of the disease is such that any recovery will be of limited duration . . . '

I looked at him, blankly. 'You mean the pneumocystis has caused permanent damage to his lungs?'

Dr Hopkin straightened up and pushed his hands into the pockets of his white coat. 'I mean, Mrs Godfrey,' he said with compassion, 'that your husband's resistance to future illness is considerably reduced.'

Along the length of corridor, ceiling lights marched in endless procession, illuminating the ubiquitous green walls and grey thermoplastic floors with a uniformity that lent them a curiously tube-like appearance. Staring, half-blindly, at the far end, I felt as if a telescope were being forcibly held to my eye.

Then the lights seemed to dim. I was peering into darkness, compelled, against my will, to see with a new perspective. And on the horizon – now visibly increasing in magnitude – was the shadowy spectre of . . .

'I . . . I don't understand . . . ' My voice came out with a croak.

Dr Hopkin leaned towards me. His forehead puckered and he appeared to be choosing his words with care.

'What I'm trying to say, Mrs Godfrey,' he said, 'is that the pneumocystis has knocked Philip's immune system back quite badly.'

* * *

On the ward, a bedpan clattered to the floor. Immediately, a bell rang shrilly, shattering the usual subdued hush; and then came the sound of feet, running . . . running . . .

Stark reality burst upon my mind. I stared at the doctor. What a fool I'd been. I had simply never put two and two together. Until that moment, I'd had no inkling that Phil's illness was associated with AIDS. I'd been too busy. Had deliberately kept myself occupied. Had refused to see what was staring me in the face.

As soon as I could, I fled for home; I could hold the tears back no longer. Unleashed, they streamed down my face whilst great cries of anguish erupted from somewhere deep inside me. Blindly, choking on a grief that had been dammed too long, I clutched Natasha's Moses basket in one hand and dashed out to the car. Somehow, I drove across town and reached the sanctuary of number seventy-three.

The moment the front door shut behind me, I plucked Natasha from her basket, hugged her against my shoulder and broke into fresh bouts of weeping. Between sobs I murmured, for all the world as if she could understand, 'Daddy's very ill. We'll have to take extra special care of him.'

Then I prepared for the long, dark hours of night.

3

The Naked Truth

'For sighing comes to me instead of food; my groans pour out like water. What I feared has come upon me, what I dreaded has happened to me.'

Job 3:24, 25

After three days, Phil was showing definite signs of improvement and it became increasingly obvious that he was responding well to the drugs. His breathing was easier and his complexion, always pale, was less grey. That weekend the family came from Sevenoaks and Gloucester to visit him in hospital and he was able to take an interest in the results of the general election – and Mrs Thatcher's third term of office. Even so, I sensed that he was depressed and when I questioned him, once we were alone, he admitted that this was so.

'I'm now officially on the List, you see.'

'What does that mean?' I asked, seating myself on a straight-back chair beside him.

'All infectious diseases are notifiable,' he explained, 'and there's a special list for AIDS sufferers. Because pneumocystis is an AIDS-related disease and I'm known to be HIV positive anyway, the hospital will have had to inform the Government of my illness.'

'Surely that information is confidential?' I asked, not sure that I fully understood the nature of his concern.

'Oh, yes, the Ministry will keep it to themselves.'

He paused, then said, 'It's just that it really depresses me to know that I'm now officially classified as having AIDS.'

I reached across the coarse white hospital sheet and grasped his hand in mine. His fingers felt thin and cold to my touch . . .

For the first time, I felt compelled to tell someone the truth about Phil's condition. Simon and Jac (Jacqueline) Gardner had been our housegroup leaders before they'd asked Phil and Richard Mason to take over from them. We were all of an age and had become good friends; when they invited me over to dinner one evening, I found myself sharing my concerns. Fear of censure still made it difficult to come right out and say 'Phil has AIDS', but by the time I had finished, they were in no doubt as to the nature and gravity of his illness.

'It's such a relief to have someone to talk to,' I said to Phil when I saw him next. 'And they couldn't have been kinder . . . '

For two weeks I visited Phil daily, arriving as early in the morning as my chores would allow, and leaving for home only when I had to in the evening. Natasha was now a month old, and I couldn't help feeling that it was a good thing she was sufficiently young and undemanding to be left to sleep in her Moses basket all day, between feeds: it gave me freedom to spend most of the time with Phil.

One evening, shortly before his release, he told me that he had been giving a great deal of thought to the future.

'What will you do, Jana, if anything happens to me?'

I pushed the last of the pinks I'd been arranging into a vase on the locker and sat down by the bed.

'Stop worrying, Boss,' I said. 'You're going to get well again.'

'Would you go back to Richmond?' he persisted. 'Or would there be too many memories . . . '

Was he worrying about where Natasha would be brought up, I wondered? Aloud, I said: 'Let's cross that bridge if and when we have to. At the moment all you have to do is to concentrate on getting well again.'

I stared at the open window on the far side of the room. Sticky humidity and overcast skies had been the order of the day throughout the month of June. Although the evening was not far advanced, daylight was already on the wane, and the sort of hush that comes before a storm hung in the still, warm air. Soon it would be time for me to leave. I focused my eyes again.

Phil turned on his side. 'I feel as if death is staring me in the face,' he said.

Abruptly, I pushed my chair back from the bed. It made a loud scraping noise on the floor.

'Stop it, honey . . . '

Quickly, he reached for my hand. 'I don't like to dwell on it,' he said, 'but we have to be realistic . . . '

'Please, Phil . . . ' Tears pricked the backs of my eyes.

'I'm sorry, dear. But it's so hard . . . Sometimes, I wonder where God is in all of this. Why me? Why me?'

I buried my head in his chest. It was a question I couldn't answer.

*　　　*　　　*

Next day, 19th June, Phil was considered well enough to be discharged. Together we sat in the nurses' room – with Natasha in her basket at our feet – for a final chat with Dr Hopkin. He briefed us as to Phil's medication and subsequent check-ups, then he paused and looked from one to the other of us.

'Do you have any questions?' he asked.

Phil cleared his throat.

'Yes. There's something I'd like to know . . . '

He stopped and took a deep breath. Dr Hopkin waited and I turned, expectantly, to look at Phil. It was evident that he was waging a battle with himself. Then he appeared to summon up an extra reserve of strength from somewhere deep within and said, quietly, 'How long? How much longer do I have?'

I swallowed hard and tried not to look away.

Dr Hopkin replied, 'The current average prognosis for someone in your condition is three years.'

'Thank you,' said Phil.

I said nothing. What was there to say?

We rose, shook hands and left the hospital.

We were silent on the journey home and, almost as a reflex action, my first instinct, when we got in, was to put the kettle on for a cup of tea. I checked Natasha, asleep in her basket, then sat next to Phil on the settee and put my arms around him.

'Why'd you ask that, hon?'

For a moment, he stared into space.

'It wasn't easy,' he admitted, with a catch in his throat. 'But I just . . . wanted to know . . . what to expect . . . '

I began to cry. The tension and worry of the last couple of weeks had taken their toll. When I thought about the three years that Dr Hopkin had given Phil . . . It was like a death sentence hanging over us.

'It'll get worse, Jana. How will you cope? You won't want to . . . '

'Honey!' It was all I could do to hold myself in check. I couldn't afford to break down like this. I had to be strong. For Phil's sake, I had to put my misery behind me; had to get him well again; had to make those three years worthwhile. There was Natasha, too . . . She needed me, as well as Phil. We all needed each other. We were a family.

I sat up, blew my nose and dried my eyes.

'Whatever happens, honey,' I said, 'I'll be with you.'

Hearing myself utter those words stiffened the resolve that was only now formulating in my mind. My voice strengthened.

'I won't leave you, Phil,' I promised. 'I'll be there – 'til the end.'

Then I got up and went to make the tea.

* * *

'Nine a week, I have to take, to keep the pneumocystis at bay.'

Phil held aloft a huge bottle of Septrin tablets that he'd been given when he'd been discharged from hospital a few days previously.

'Trouble is,' he continued, 'I've now got a bad case of thrush.'

Phil never sat if he could lounge and I often complained that he wore the seat of his jeans through before the knee showed signs of wear. True to form, he was sprawled on the settee with his legs hanging over the end, watching cricket on TV.

'Let me look,' I said, and pushed my knitting behind me in the chair. I crouched beside him.

Obligingly, he opened his mouth and I peered down his throat. A white, curdlike deposit coated his tongue and the inside of his cheeks. It looked disgusting.

'It's one of the side effects of the Septrin,' he explained when I wrinkled my nose and backed off. 'Antibiotics can't discriminate between different bacteria. As well as the infection, they kill off the yeasts that naturally inhabit the digestive system and keep everything else in check. Then you get this fungus . . . '

'How revolting. Is it sore?'

He nodded, swallowed painfully and sat up. 'It's damned uncomfortable. And there's not a lot they can do except pump me full of antifungal drugs or give me mouth-washes.'

'Doesn't that help?'

He made a wry face. 'As soon as you take them, the effect's wiped out by the Septrin. Catch twenty-two.'

'What you need is a good holiday,' I said, sitting myself down and taking up my knitting again. 'I think it might be a good idea if we took your parents up on their offer of help . . . '

When Phil had gone into hospital, Mum and Dad had made what we considered a most generous suggestion: 'If we let you have the money, you could go to Australia together when Phil's conference comes up. Extend it – make it a proper trip. It'll do you both good.'

Phil had felt somewhat diffident about accepting an outright gift from his parents but eventually it was agreed that they would loan us the money against his inheritance. Towards the end of August we set off with Natasha on a world trip.

'It'll be quite an undertaking,' Phil's mother warned me.

Believing that it might be the last opportunity we would have to travel so extensively I made light of any fears I might have had on that score. And in the event, there was no need to worry. Daily, I watched Phil's health improve and though we had fixed a fairly gruelling itinerary, taking in a visit to Singapore, Hawaii and, finally, the USA to visit my family, he coped admirably and the break was beneficial to us both.

We'd arranged that I would stay on in the States for a further two weeks after Phil's departure, so it was mid-September before we were once more installed in our little house in Percy Street. Restored in health and spirit, we were totally unprepared for the turn of events that engulfed us later that autumn.

*　　*　　*

During the years of my marriage to Phil, I had learned a good deal about haemophilia and knew that it was an inherited condition – though it could, as in Phil's case, appear in a family with no apparent history of a bleeding disorder. Haemophilia affects only men and is inherited via an abnormal X chromosome. A man has only one X chromosome plus one Y. Since all his sons inherit only the Y chromosome from him (and the X from their mother) it follows that *none* of the sons of a haemophiliac will suffer from the condition themselves (unless their mother is a carrier).

Females are made up of two X chromosomes – one from each parent. Because the only X chromosome from a haemophiliac father is defective, *all* his daughters will be carriers.

Carriers have a fifty-fifty chance of having normal, unaffected children. Babies born to them may inherit their normal X chromosome and be in the clear. However, if the abnormal X is passed on, then the girls will be carriers and the boys haemophiliacs.

Peter Godfrey was not a haemophiliac and – short of testing – there was no way of knowing whether Phil's sister, Paulette, was a carrier or not. Her husband, David Maxted, was a doctor and was, therefore, fully aware of the risk. Prior to their marriage, he had insisted – as a measure of his love for his bride – that Paulette should not be subjected to a test. He did not want her to feel that his love for her was conditional, nor that she was in any way defective.

Two or three months later, however, blood samples had revealed her to be a carrier. Despite that, David and Paulette had agreed, when she became pregnant, that there should be no ante-natal testing to determine whether the foetus was affected or not. They believed that, whatever the outcome, God was in control. And when Andrew, their eldest son, had been born unaffected, any fears that they might have harboured about perpetuating the defect had receded.

It had been a shock, therefore, when their second son, James, had been born in March, 1987, to discover that he was a haemophiliac. Reeling under an enormous burden of irrational guilt, Paulette had been devastated. However, worse was to come. That November, when James was barely eight months old, we heard from Phil's parents that he had been taken into hospital.

'He has SCIDS,' Phil's dad told us. 'Severe Combined Immune Deficiency Syndrome.'

Little was known of the condition. Only that it was a congenital illness and was extremely rare. What could not be disputed was that whilst Phil's immune system was slowly deteriorating, Baby James had been found to have none at all.

*   *   *

After James' illness, the winter of '87 passed relatively uneventfully. Towards the end of May in the following year, Phil's working schedule made increased demands upon his time and energies. Once more, he had responsibility for two medical students who were involved in projects under his jurisdiction. In addition, he was preparing for a conference in Perugia, Italy as well as attending frequent interviews for a new situation.

'My grant runs out soon,' he explained. 'I have to keep applying for jobs elsewhere.'

'Well, I'm fed up with it,' I complained one evening when he was late home for supper for the third time that week. 'We hardly get to see one another these days.'

'It can't be helped, Boss. It wouldn't augur well for the future if I fall down on the job now.'

I knew that what he said made sense but still I sulked.

'It's not as if you get paid big bucks. Seems to me that for all the kudos supposedly attached to academia, they expect an awful lot in return for the pittance you're paid.'

'I did tell you before we married that we'd never be wealthy,' Phil said, patiently.

'We could be – if only . . . '

'Now, Jana! You know I love what I'm doing.'

'But how d'you know you wouldn't get just as much out of industry?' I retorted.

I hated myself for being so churlish. Phil was obviously under pressure and I knew that he wasn't sleeping well. Though I knew it to be futile and irrational, somehow I just couldn't stop myself from lashing out at him, as the cause of all my grievances. Like an immature child, I was taking out my hurts and fears on the very person whom I most loved and upon whom my fears were centred. Deep down, I knew that I was hurting Phil because he was the source of my own hurt. What sort of Christian witness was this? Guilt compounded my misery.

'I want another baby,' I said, sullenly, 'but if you keep applying for such dead-end jobs we'll never be able to afford it.'

'It's not just a case of *affording* another baby, Boss . . . There is the health problem . . . '

'Oh, Phil! We've been through all that . . . It's *my* health we're talking about.'

For hours, Phil and I argued the toss, with me sulking and moody and he alternately cajoling and reasoning.

Eventually after some weeks, Phil, with characteristic patience, began actively applying for employment outside his own narrow sphere. And we agreed to enlarge our family.

'But it's your decision, not mine,' he said, firmly.

Secretly, I was cross with him for putting the onus on me and felt let down, in that he failed to understand the importance of this baby to me. Panic set in whenever I considered the fact that there might come a time – possibly in the not too distant future – when Phil would be too ill to father a second child. The near certainty of that prognosis was more than I could bear and I was filled with despair. Fuelled with such morbid introspection, I determined to press ahead whilst I had Phil's co-operation, regardless of whether or not I had his full blessing.

I spoke at length with Linda Jones and Mary Fletcher at the Haemophilia Centre. Mary was a senior social worker, a big, rosy-faced woman with brown chin-length curly hair. Older than Linda, though with the same degree of sympathy for my situation, she advised me on the optimum conditions for conception.

'Obviously, we can't eliminate the risks of unprotected sexual intercourse,' she explained, 'but they can be minimised. You need to establish the most fertile period of your cycle, Jana. To do that you need to take your temperature regularly at the same time each day.'

She showed me how to get an accurate thermometer reading and how to keep a chart of my findings.

'At least then you won't be prolonging the risk,' she concluded. 'You can confine your love-making to those times when you'll be most likely to conceive straight away.'

Carefully following her instructions, I pinpointed 5th June as mid-ovulation in my cycle and informed Phil that this was the peak time for conception to take place. Immediately, we began trying for a baby – a brother or sister for Natasha.

The following morning, Phil awoke with double vision.

*   *   *

'I've been having blinding headaches for some time,' Phil admitted, when I questioned him.

In fact, he had been taking paracetamol every three hours throughout the duration of his last conference, in Italy. Alarmed, I telephoned the Haemophilia Centre at the Churchill Hospital and when Phil went in later that day, they ran a series of tests on him.

'I'm afraid it's meningitis,' Dr Rizza diagnosed, and made immediate arrangements for Phil to be admitted.

Four days later, after being put on a course of amphotericin, delivered intravenously, Phil was allowed home. I collected him from the hospital in the car.

'But I'm going to have to go back in, periodically, for treatment,' he said as we drove off.

Things seemed to be accelerating faster than I could keep up with them. We were due to go away with Phil's family in less than a fortnight.

'What about our holiday in Scotland?' I asked when I'd negotiated my way across town and had time to digest the news.

'You can still go,' Phil said.

'By myself?'

'You'll have Tash.'

'You know what I mean, honey. I can't leave you at home on your own.'

'You go,' Phil insisted. 'I shall be perfectly okay. The hospital will be keeping tabs on me.'

It was with mixed feelings that I drove the Maxi – Frank the Tank as I derisively called it – down Percy Street, and parked outside our little house.

*   *   *

Phil stayed at home whilst Natasha and I joined his parents and Trina in Scotland and other than admitting to a sense of loneliness, he suffered no ill effects. Shortly after this, a new drug called Fluconazol was marketed, and as this was active against a wide range of fungal infections, it did a great job of clearing away the thrush. From then on it was prescribed as a preventative measure.

In August, 1988, Phil was well enough to attend a conference in Munich where I was able to join him, leaving Tasha with her grandma. Afterwards, we went on a whirlwind tour – in what Phil teasingly called 'a frenzied Woldt style', as opposed to 'a restful Godfrey style' – of several of the bordering European countries. I knew that he was pushing himself for my sake, and was grateful to him for giving me this opportunity to travel. I knew instinctively, too, that the more he fought his disease the better; that the will to live is, to some extent, life sustaining.

In the meantime, Phil had regular appointments, every three weeks, with Dr Peto, Consultant Physician at the Infectious Diseases Unit of the John Warin Ward. Willingly – despite its relatively unproven record – he started a course of AZT, the new anti-AIDS drug that was receiving so much media attention as the hoped-for saviour.

Whatever its merits – and the number of pills that Phil was taking increased daily – we still put *our* trust in the

Lord. Not that there was anything great or overt about our faith. No grand gestures or miracle cures. Just a quiet and simple belief that no matter what befell us, God would see us through; and that by His presence with us, we would be strengthened to endure to the end.

That faith, however, though buried deep within, was not always apparent in my behaviour. We were still trying for a baby and I was bitterly disappointed to discover, each month, that I had failed to become pregnant. There was an urgency in my despair. By early September, when my sister Wendy and her husband Mike came to visit with their toddler, Tawny, the passage of time had already made tremendous inroads into Phil's life expectancy. Here was Tasha, just taking her first steps with her cousin Tawny, and already her daddy's life was running out – fast, like twilight on a winter's day. Of the three years he had been given, fifteen months had elapsed. Gone! Never to come again.

More than one year down. Less than two to go. *If* we were lucky. These last months could never be recalled and I felt driven by some subconscious force to reproduce life. Phil's life. Flesh of his flesh.

Tired and depressed, I was not always able to manifest the peace of God that He promises to those who travail.

'Sometimes I get the feeling,' said Phil, after yet another night of waking me with his incessant coughing, 'that you blame me?'

Blinking in the sudden glare from the bedroom light, I was too weary to be bothered to reply. Next day, however, I considered his accusation.

'I think you're right,' I admitted. 'However irrational it is to blame you, your cough really grates on my nerves.'

'Haven't you got used to it yet?' Phil asked.

I shook my head, emphatically. 'How can I? It's a constant reminder to me of how ill you are. And how worried I am about you.'

And about having another baby, I thought. But I didn't mention that aloud.

Phil's job with the University Department of Clinical Pharmacology was based at the Radcliffe Infirmary, not too far from home. Fortunately, science allows for a flexible schedule and though, generally, his health had been fairly good, on mornings when he felt tired, he had simply been able to go into work later. With the return of his cough, however, he began to feel ill again. Too ill for sex. Too ill to make another baby. And too ill for the news we'd all dreaded.

On 13th November, 1988, after numerous tests and treatments and a valiant fight for life, baby James Maxted died. He was twenty months old. His death brought home to me, like nothing else could, the transient nature of life.

4

No Darkness Too Black

'But He knows the way that I take; when He has tested me I shall come forth as gold.'

Job 23:10

Our social workers called regularly from the Haemophilia Centre to take a sample of my blood for testing at the hospital, and to talk through any issues that were bothering Phil and me. One day in early November, when a thin grey drizzle greased the pavements of Percy Street, Mary Fletcher came to see me. Parking in the vicinity was hard to find and it was evident that she'd had to walk some distance from her car. Her dark hair was slicked to her head and rain beaded her eyelashes and nose.

'What a day!' she complained, wiping the moisture from her face, but her round, fleshy features were wreathed in smiles that belied any ill humour. As soon as she was in, and had dried off as best she could, she dispensed with the blood-letting.

'Get this out of the way first, then we can relax,' she said, swabbing my outstretched arm then swiftly puncturing a vein. Throughout the procedure, she kept up a steady stream of patter which, I had no doubt, was intended to put me at ease.

'How are you feeling in yourself?' she asked when we were at last settled in the front room, she on the sofa and

I slouched on a beat-up armchair that had once belonged to Mum and Dad.

I shrugged. 'Okay, I s'pose.'

Silence ensued. Tasha was asleep upstairs in her cot and only the hiss of the gasfire filled the room. Mary's face softened. I looked away, clinging to my natural diffidence, but it was no good. I knew I couldn't fool her.

'No, I'm not! I'm still not pregnant. We're struggling to make ends meet financially. And Phil's job prospects don't look up to much.' Miserably, I blinked back the tears that sprang to my eyes.

Mary clucked, sympathetically. 'What sort of job is Phil after?'

I picked up a piece of tapestry I had been working on and hid my emotions in a meticulous examination of the stitching. 'He's been for an interview for a lectureship. It would be a more permanent post than the one he has now . . . ' I stabbed a needle in and out of the canvas.

'Well, that's good that he's had an interview, isn't it?' Mary asked, in tones of optimism.

'Yes . . . But . . . It's in academia again. And it's so badly paid.'

'Can't you talk about it together?'

'Oh, we do.' I knew from Mary that communication between some of the couples that she visited was almost non-existent. There were those, she said, who had not even been able to bring themselves to tell their spouses that they were HIV positive. Knowing that, gave me a perverse sense of encouragement. Whatever problems Phil and I had to face, we at least faced them together.

'I never push Phil in any way,' I continued. 'I just ask him to keep an open mind about applying for jobs in industry.'

'And how does he feel about that?'

I considered for a moment. 'Well,' I said, slowly, 'I guess having more money is less important to him than the freedom he enjoys now.'

'Do you think he'll find something nearby?' Mary asked.

I knew that she became very attached to 'her' patients and families and hated them moving away from the area. Some of them lived hundreds of miles from the Centre and travelled in whenever they were in need of treatment – one from as far as the Isle of Wight. It was my turn to encourage her.

'Something'll turn up,' I said. 'There's certainly no hope of us ever being able to move back to the States to be near my family.'

Even holidays there were proving difficult. The US Government demanded that if a person were HIV positive, that fact should be stated on their passport. Phil vigorously refused to comply: 'It's none of their business,' he would say, knowing full well that to declare his condition was to risk being denied entry to the country.

Still, I knew that there was a restlessness in me. I was ready for change. Apart from the fact that many of our friends were in the process of changing jobs and homes, I had a feeling that it might be easier to start over again. Then we wouldn't have the embarrassment of explaining away Phil's physical deterioration to people who knew us well.

We had kept the fact that Phil had AIDS a deep dark secret from friends and colleagues, other than Simon and Jac. It wasn't a policy we'd actually discussed; more of a mute decision, assiduously encouraged by Dr Rizza. I suppose, too, if I were honest, that I didn't like to think too closely about what sort of reaction we might receive if we did disclose Phil's condition. How would neighbours respond if they knew that they were living next door to an AIDS sufferer, I wondered? Would we become social outcasts – the modern-day equivalent of lepers? And what of Tasha when she started playschool? If it became known that her daddy had the dreaded virus, would parents ask for her removal?

The wider family would be okay, I was sure, *and* probably most of the folk with whom Phil worked. After all, they were scientists and would know that AIDS was neither infectious nor contagious. Phil had explained that to me once. 'Contagious' referred to illness that could be passed from one person to another by bodily contact, whilst 'infectious' meant that which could be transmitted by air. AIDS fell into neither category. The only known means of transference of the virus from one human being to another was via the blood or semen of the infected person.

That, however, raised another spectre. Once it became apparent that Phil was ill, would people who didn't know us put two and two together and make five? Hysteria about the disease being what it was, suspicions would undoubtedly run riot. I didn't want Phil being thought a drug addict, an adulterer, or bisexual.

'Well . . . ' Mary stood, ready to leave. 'I'll let you know the result of this as soon as it's ready.' She patted her holdall, in which lay the phial of my blood which would be tested for the AIDS virus on her return to the Centre. 'Shouldn't be longer than a week,' she said. 'And if you're sticking to the routine of unprotected sex only at peak fertility times, I wouldn't think there'd be any problem . . . '

I opened the door and let her out into the dank November gloom.

'Hope not,' I said, and shut the door. Then I turned back to the empty room. If I was infected with the AIDS virus, I reflected as Tasha woke, that would be the last straw. It was a depressing thought.

*   *   *

It was inevitable, I suppose, that James' death should have affected us deeply. Although, as Christians, we believed in Life Eternal, and knew that he was safe with the Lord, it would be hypocritical to say that we did not mourn. The sight of Tash toddling across the floor towards me, or the warmth of her arms about my neck as she told me, 'Love 'oo, Mummy', could not fail to rouse within me the most profound compassion for Paulette and David in their loss. And yet the question, Why? was simply not a part of my vocabulary. Others might rail against God for the suffering and death of the world – particularly that of a helpless baby; but it never occurred to Phil and me to do other than accept, with equanimity, the Father-love of God. And the depression that we experienced in the following months was simply the natural outworking of an accumulation of stressful situations.

The results of my AIDS test were negative, yet I was filled with a grey lassitude that dragged me from bed each morning and drove me to seek oblivion in sleep each night. Only our Christmas visit home to America, and the usual hectic itinerary of sightseeing in New York, Boston, Niagara and Toronto fuelled my energies and kept at bay the worst of my spectres.

We returned home mid-January.

One day, late in February, we were all seated at the breakfast table. We made a good-looking family group, I thought, fondly. Seated in her highchair, Tasha looked so cute, her white-blonde hair gleaming softly in the tungsten light, her mouth a bright bow of red. Most people said she looked like me, but her fairness was definitely Phil's.

He sat at her side, keeping an attentive eye on the destination of each spoonful of cereal with which his daughter was attempting to feed herself. When appropriate – which was frequently, for Tasha was a messy eater – he mopped up.

He wore his favourite shrunken red and white striped jumper, and for the umpteenth time I resolved that I really must knit him another to replace it. The sleeves were pushed up on his forearms in the usual way, and his feet were shod with basketball boots, loosely laced above the ankle. Phil never wore conventional footwear if he could help it; leather chafed joints made tender by bleeds, and shoes gave him no support.

I poured a bowl of Shreddies for Phil, then turned to get on with my own breakfast. I loved food and would happily eat at any time. The dictates of my appetite tended to be on the basis of desire rather than real stomach hunger. Phil, by contrast, ate little and infrequently, masticating each bite slowly and swallowing with difficulty. He found my ongoing 'battle of the bulge' totally incomprehensible, and though supportive, he had strong views as to his preferences.

'I like to be able to feel your bones and see your waistline,' he would tell me. And here I was gaining weight.

We were not generally a talkative family in the mornings so for some moments I didn't realise that Phil was having problems. When I looked up from my plate, I saw that he was sitting very upright and rigid, a frown on his face, as if concentrating hard. I watched him. With his tongue, he was poking around inside his mouth, whilst between the thumb and forefinger of his right hand he held something too small for me to make it out.

'What's the matter?' I asked, when he offered no explanation.

'I'm not sure.'

Tasha looked at her daddy with interest and made some remark in her usual unintelligible manner.

'Is it a filling?' I asked.

Phil paused in his exploration to examine the particle in his hand then said, 'I think Tash is right. It's a tooth.'

'Probably just a bit of hard grain in your cereal,' I replied.

'I don't think so.' He peered at it again. 'Nope!' he said. 'That's definitely a bit of tooth.'

I leaned across the table. There was no mistaking the creamy-grey enamel that lay in Phil's hand.

Suddenly, I was consumed with fear. From the outside Phil's body looked normal. It had never occurred to me to speculate on what was going on inside. Yet who knew the extent of deterioration that had already taken place? Flesh, bones and blood vessels; kidneys, liver and heart: were they all shrinking and crumbling away?

Oh, Lord, I breathed silently, slumping back in my chair, is Phil's body breaking down bit by bit?

From her highchair, Tasha tutted and reached out, as if to commiserate with her daddy that whilst her young body was full of health and vigour, his was taken over with decay.

'Me see?' she demanded. And clutching at the hand that held his tooth, she began to prise open his fingers. One, by one, by one.

* * *

More depressed than ever, I turned increasingly to food for comfort. My weight began to spiral upward, out of control; the more I gained, the deeper grew my depression and the greater my need of compensation. The 'trials' that Dad had prayed us through when we'd first known of Phil's condition, three and a half years previously, seemed to be piling up thick and fast. A fortnight after the tooth incident, another unrelated event knocked me sideways.

We were sitting at home one evening, when the telephone rang. As Phil was absorbed in a fantasy movie on TV, I set down my tapestry, went through to the dining-room and picked up the receiver.

'Hi, Jana! It's Paulette.'

There was a hint of suppressed excitement in the voice of Phil's eldest sister, and as a telephone conversation with her was always a lengthy and enjoyable affair, I seated myself at the table.

'Phil's not watching TV *again*, is he?' Paulette teased.

For some moments we engaged in a dialogue of banter. Then a lull occurred. It was heavy with innuendo.

'Guess what?' Paulette exclaimed, breaking the silence.

It was hard to resist her vivacious good humour and in spite of my low spirits, I found myself responding.

'What's happened?' I asked.

'I've missed two months, and . . . ' She paused, dramatically.

'Missed two months?'

I coiled the telephone flex round my hand, released it, then ironed out the kinks with my fingers. Slowly, my mind assimilated the information that Paulette had imparted. There was an acute sense of reluctance on my part to accept what I knew to be true.

'Two months?' I repeated. 'You're not . . . ?'

'Yes! Eleven weeks . . . '

A leaden shadow leered at the window. It was only that of a creeper against the wall, but my throat tightened. Paulette is pregnant, my mind cried. Pregnant. Pregnant. Pregnant.

With some difficulty I formulated the appropriate, expected response.

'That's great . . . When's it due?'

'October. Around your birthday.'

Gladly, Paulette elaborated. I hardly heard. Eventually, we said goodbye. I set the receiver down carefully on its cradle and stared into space, grappling with the images aroused by her news.

She had blamed herself for James' demise, convinced, despite a lack of evidence, that she was responsible for passing on the SCID syndrome. Understandably, she had been racked with fear by thoughts of the risks attached to any future pregnancy. Nevertheless, she had an overwhelming desire for another child.

At last, persuaded by prayer and by medical rhetoric that a recurrence of the rare fatal condition was highly unlikely, Paulette had succumbed to faith and reason. Though still burdened with guilt at the possibility of perpetuating the haemophilia disorder, she had decided, with David's blessing, to increase their family.

Even before the event, the reaction of friends had been varied. There were those who had shown undisguised disapprobation. Others had expressed compassion, and supported her yearning for another baby.

That yearning was something with which I could identify. As I sat by the phone, I was sick with envy. Paulette

had achieved what I had not. And I was weighed down
with the guilt of my unworthy thoughts.

'Forgive me, Lord,' I prayed silently, 'and help me not
to be jealous.'

For some moments I struggled to regain my composure.
Then I dragged myself to my feet, returned to the front
room and slumped into my chair.

'Who was that?' Phil asked, turning his attention
momentarily away from the television.

'Paulette,' I said, briefly.

'News?'

'Yeah.' I picked up my canvas.

'Are she and David okay?'

'Fine.' I pulled a length of green wool from a skein.
Then I said, 'She's pregnant.'

And brandishing the scissors, I cut swift and clean
through the thread.

                    *   *   *

Next day was Phil's birthday, and the following week he
was DJ at a sixties dance given by the fellowship groups
in our area. I wore a yellow mini skirt, emblazoned with
pink and green stylised flowers, that revealed an immense
length of black fishnet stockings, and I made every effort
to enter into the gaiety of the evening. Paulette's news
appeared to have little effect on Phil and I had no
option but to work through my potentially damaging
emotions alone. As far as I could see, he simply had no
understanding of my longing for a baby.

The following day, Phil had an introductory gliding
lesson that I'd given him as a gift for his birthday. However, whilst he soared above the Oxfordshire countryside
and revelled in the experience, I was well and truly
earthbound, dug in and entrenched in my depression.
Desperately, I prayed for God's help.

For our fifth wedding anniversary at the end of the
month, we took a trip to Florence, where Phil had a

scientific meeting. The occasion provided a much needed opportunity for me to escape from my negative thought patterns, by indulging me in the all-American national pastime of Shopping and Sightseeing. The change, as they say, was as good as a rest. Our last night was spent in Paris and, finally armed with the strength and determination to pull myself together, I was able again to face the disappointments of life at home.

Then one evening in May, when all the evidence of creation promised newness and hope, it seemed that the Lord had heard my prayers.

'How would this suit you?' Phil asked, plonking himself down on the settee next to me and producing a copy of *Nature* magazine. He indicated a small advertisement inviting applications for a biochemist specialising in pharmaceutical research, and waited while I skimmed through it to the end.

'Geneva?' I exclaimed, scrutinising him carefully to see if he was teasing.

'I thought that would appeal! It's the Glaxo Institute for Molecular Biology.'

This was Phil's field. Avidly, I studied the fine print. The job sounded tailor-made. Restraining a growing sense of excitement, I asked, cautiously, 'Are you gonna go for it?'

He grinned. 'They'd never take me on . . . '

'How d'you know unless you apply?'

'Jana, I do know . . . '

'It couldn't do any harm to write. You've had no offers here so you've nothing to lose.'

'But even if they liked my application . . . Even if I got past an interview . . . Be serious, Boss. How could we go to Geneva?'

I put the open magazine on Phil's lap, with the advert uppermost.

'Go on,' I said flippantly. 'Why don't you try . . . ' And I went to the kitchen to prepare dinner, dreaming of Swiss Alps, Suchard chocolate and musical boxes.

Faith is the hope of things unseen and when Phil decided
to take the first step in applying for the job, I found my
spirits lifting. And with my newfound optimism came a
corresponding stiffening of my resolve to take control of
my life once more.

'Something's clicked inside me,' I said to Phil. 'I'm
determined to get some discipline back into my eating again. So I've made up my mind to join Weight
Watchers.'

Phil grinned and gave me a hug. 'It'll be nice to be able to
get my arms around you again,' he teased. 'I was beginning
to think a divorce would be on the cards and that I'd have
to swap you for a slimmer model.'

Next day, I took myself off and joined the Oxford class
at Headington. From my lecturer, Annette, I learned that
my Goal Weight was eight stone seven and that in order to
reach it, I had about twenty pounds to lose. Resolutely, I
gritted my teeth.

*   *   *

'Nanash,' I said delightedly to Phil six weeks later, when
we had packed up our red Ford Escort and were on
our way to join the Godfrey family in a rented house
in Solva, on the Pembrokeshire coast in Wales. 'That's
what Natasha calls herself. Nanash. Don't you think
that's cute?'

Our little daughter was growing fast and Phil was as
besotted with his 'Squiddly Diddly' as I. He spent hours
bathing her and reading to her, but sadly, he tired too
quickly to spend much time in the rough and tumble
play which had been a hallmark of his courtship of me.
Nevertheless, opportunities, I hoped, might evolve out of
our vacation.

Phil's gran was one of the holiday party, along with
Pat and Peter – Phil's mum and dad – and Patrina, his
youngest sister.

'Wonder when Paulette will be able to join us?' I

asked, remembering that, at the last minute, Andrew, her five-year-old, had come out in spots. With characteristic thoughtfulness, she had checked with Dr Rizza at the Haemophilia Centre, to discover if contact could be detrimental to Phil.

'He said that any illness – even a childhood ailment like chicken-pox – could have disastrous effects in knocking back Phil's immune system,' she told us. 'I'll just have to come over later.'

In the event, it was not until the final couple of days that she was able to join the rest of the party. AIDS, I was learning, had far-reaching effects.

* * *

Our social workers still visited frequently. One day, towards the end of July, Linda Jones popped in to take blood samples from me and to encourage me with a friendly chat. I always enjoyed her company and drew strength from hearing how other couples were coping in similar circumstances to our own.

'How's Phil?' she asked.

'He's as determined as ever to enjoy life to the full,' I replied. 'We had to cut our holiday short so that he could go to La Scala cinema in London for an all-night horror film festival.'

Linda and I were sitting out in the tiny back garden of number seventy-three, enjoying the last of the day's sun. The lawn that Phil and his father had sown five years earlier, was showing signs of wear from Tasha's toys, and the roses that cascaded over the fence were past their best. Even so, it was a small oasis of tranquillity in the midst of Oxford's city life and the air was redolent with summer scents.

Linda sniffed appreciatively. 'Phil's incredible,' she said, making no attempt to hide her admiration. 'I think he showed me a poster of the festival, some time ago. Didn't it have a catchy sort of title?'

'Shock Around the Clock,' I replied, and turned in response to Tasha's bellows from behind me. One wheel of the fire engine she was riding was lodged in the gulley from the drain, and she had evidently taken a tumble.

'Up you get, Pumpkin,' I said, calmly. I never rushed to her aid when she fell and she was fast becoming an independent little girl. Occasionally, it occurred to me to wonder if I was selfish. Other mothers seemed to adopt a much fussier attitude to their children.

Linda crossed the patio, retrieved the little red fire engine, dusted Tash off and brought her over.

'Here,' she said, taking a chocolate drop from her handbag and offering it to Natasha. Tash was instantly mollified. Then Linda turned to me. 'Phil never lets his illness get him down, does he?' she said. 'It must make life easier for you. I know other couples who've given up on everything.'

I thought for a moment. 'I do sometimes wonder if I'd have Phil's courage in similar circumstances.'

'I'm sure you would,' Linda said. 'Anyone can see what a strength you are to him.'

'I don't always feel it,' I admitted. 'Sometimes I feel totally inadequate.'

'Well, you don't come across like that,' she assured me. 'You seem to have a . . . an inner calm. And that's just what he'll need. He's bound to be down at times, as the illness progresses.'

I felt greatly encouraged. Our curate, Rod Symmons, and a couple of people from church, had formed themselves into a group when Phil had gone down with pneumocystis, and had committed themselves to regular prayer. We met, in that respect, every six months and on the last occasion I had asked their opinion on how I should pray.

'I don't know whether to ask just for wisdom for the doctors and strength for myself and Phil, or whether I should be asking for complete healing for him,' I'd confessed. 'I guess I'm a little afraid that if Phil wasn't healed, I might become bitter and angry with God. And I don't want to risk that.'

Rod had been confident. 'I think we should pray for total healing, Jana. God wants His children whole.'

His response had left me ambivalent. Sometimes I'd wondered if some unresolved sin on my part had rendered the group's prayers for healing ineffective. Now, however, Linda's observation seemed to indicate that God was indeed strengthening both Phil and me – if not physically, then mentally, emotionally and spiritually.

Three days later, I learned from Annette, my Weight Watchers lecturer, that I was only two pounds off reaching my Goal Weight. Taking this as further evidence of my ability to cope, I put it to Phil, when we went to bed that night, that we should again start trying for another baby.

'You're feeling well, at present,' I said. 'And it would be a reward for me, for losing all my weight.'

Laughing at my rhetoric, he gladly complied.

At that precise moment, I didn't think it prudent to remind him that we had an appointment the following week at the Fertility Clinic.

*   *   *

'No, my blood test's normal, Mom,' I said into the telephone, lapsing into the broad American drawl I'd all but eliminated since my marriage to Phil. 'And we're seeing the people at the Radcliffe . . . '

Although I rang my mother frequently, there were some things that I found too embarrassing to discuss with her. Consequently, I couldn't bring myself to mention that prior to our appointment, Phil was to undergo a sperm count and that he wasn't at all keen. Nor that he still didn't seem to understand how important it was to me to have another baby.

The front door opened and I looked up in surprise. Phil stood in the aperture. He was not ordinarily home this early and my immediate thought was that he was ill again. Hastily, I bade my mom goodbye and put the phone down.

Phil certainly didn't look unwell; in fact, if anything, he looked positively exuberant.

'Guess what . . . ' He grinned, mischievously.

'What's happened?' I asked.

Deliberately winding me up he said, 'Have I got news for you . . . '

'Oh, come on, Boss. Tell . . . '

'Ta da!' With a flourish, he pulled out an envelope and brandished it above my head. Snatching it from him, I began to read.

'Wow!' I said. And with a mounting sense of excitement I sank down on to the settee. The letter that I held in my hand was from Glaxo IMB. They had invited Phil for an interview in Geneva.

*   *   *

Bright evening sunlight flooded the sitting-room and washed the walls with a warm glow reflected from the russet carpet. A few late roses, vivid splotches of scarlet and caramel, spilled from a vase on the shelf and strewed an extravagant carpet of petals round about. In the still summer air, their perfume was a heady cocktail.

'Geneva!' I gasped. 'Just think!'

Phil raised his eyebrows. 'It's ages since I applied . . . I'd forgotten . . . '

'Let's see. April, wasn't it?' I totted up on my fingers. 'Four months. They've taken their time.'

'I expect they've had masses of applicants.'

'So what happens now?'

'They've asked me to fly out.'

'That's great! I told you to go for it. You were so reluctant.'

'It's only an interview.'

'Right! But you never know . . . '

'I won't get the job . . . '

'At least it's a trip to Geneva!' I turned, scooped up the fallen rose petals in my hands and sniffed their bouquet. 'Think positive. Even if nothing comes of it, you'll have seen the Alps.'

'Okay! Why not? I'll ring them tomorrow.'

An appointment had been made for Phil and me to speak with Mr David Barlow, a Consultant at the Radcliffe Fertility Clinic, on 22nd August, so arrangements were made for Phil to fly out to Geneva the following day. It was difficult to know which event was uppermost in my mind in the intervening period, and the next week and a half passed in nervous anticipation.

Mr Barlow was a tall, distinguished-looking man, with greying hair and an air of authority that inspired confidence. In the half hour that we spent with him in one of the consulting rooms on the ground floor of the maternity wing, he outlined four methods of monitored conception which were currently in use in the treatment of infertile couples. Once he had ascertained that I had experienced no problem in conceiving Natasha, he was able to advise that the best method for us would probably be the monitoring of ovulation, which would mean my attending monthly appointments at the hospital.

'However,' he said, 'I'm sure you would agree that there are certain physical implications that have to be considered. I have a moral obligation to consult with my staff before we could set anything in operation, to be sure that they understand the risks and would be willing to expose themselves to them.'

When we'd finished with Mr Barlow, we went to the Churchill Hospital for Phil's regular two-weekly appointment, then next door to the Haemophilia Centre to pick up more Factor VIII to take with him to Geneva. By the time I had dropped him off at work in the afternoon, I was too tired to pack for his trip.

Next morning, I had an appointment with my GP, Dr Stevens, so Phil, deprived of the car and my chauffeurage, took a lunchtime coach to Heathrow airport to await his flight to Geneva. Throughout the day, he filled my mind and was the focus of my prayers. Every application he had made for lectureships and grants had met, so far, with closed doors. Although we only ever allowed ourselves to think in the short-term, my hope was that through this interview with Glaxo IMB, God would open up new job opportunities for him. Then together we might be able to embark upon a new life in Switzerland, for whatever time was left to us.

To pass the evening, I baked shortbread to give to Eve and Bill, our neighbours across the street who were moving the following day, then I rang my mom and had a long chat with her, followed by another with Phil's mum. At last, at nine o'clock that evening, the telephone rang again. It was Phil. He sounded nervous.

'Hi, Boss! Is everything okay?'

'Fine,' I replied. 'Where are you?'

'Hôtel de la Paix. They've pulled out all the stops. It's five-star luxury – right beside the lake. I can see the *jet d'eau* from my room.'

'Sounds like fun. Wish I was there.'

'You'd love Geneva. It's really warm here. And it's full of chocolate shops!'

I ignored his teasing and reminded him of the promise I'd extracted from him prior to his departure. 'Did you get my present yet?'

At the other end of the line, Phil chortled. 'First thing I did. Life wouldn't be worth living if I came back empty handed.'

I smiled to myself. Phil wasn't good at remembering to buy presents when he was away on a trip, unless given more than a gentle hint.

'How did your doctor's appointment go?' he asked.

'Oh, Phil! He wasn't very happy.'

'You mean he doesn't think we should try for another baby? I did say . . . '

'No, no. He was very supportive. Very understanding. He just didn't like the fact that I'd been referred to Mr

Barlow by Dr Rowland-Jones from the Churchill. He felt
that as my GP, he should have initiated the contact,
that's all.'

We talked some more, then I wished him well and
hung up. My concentration in the romantic movie I'd
been watching on TV – a penchant not shared with Phil
– was gone, ousted by matters more profound.

I didn't like Phil voicing his concerns about the health
risks attached to unprotected sex. He just didn't seem to
understand how important it was to me to have a second
child – his child. Deep down, however, though I'd said
nothing to him, I'd begun to have second thoughts myself.
Somehow, during our interview with Mr Barlow the previous day, doubts had crept in, and in the secret recesses
of my mind – barely acknowledged to my consciousness –
I had had a feeling that Geneva and another baby were
mutually exclusive.

Now, settling myself on the sofa, I was almost certain.
This was God's word for me: we wouldn't be able to do
both. It was one or the other. All that remained was to
sort out which I wanted most. Earnestly, I hoped that the
Lord would make the decision for me.

*   *   *

Phil returned from Geneva at eight-thirty on the Thursday
evening, bursting with enthusiasm for all that he'd learned.
The Glaxo Institute for Molecular Biology (GIMB), based
in Geneva, was involved in identifying new molecular
targets, against which specific drugs could be developed,
he told me. Scientists from over twenty different countries made up a workforce which was both creative and
dynamic, and good links had been established between
the Institute and other research centres in Britain, as well
as leading universities around the world, with whom they
collaborated on various research projects.

'Molecular biology is seen as an increasingly important
tool in the search for new ways of treating serious diseases,

such as Alzheimer's, Parkinson's and schizophrenia,' he said over dinner that evening. 'What Glaxo want is the intellectual input of biochemists into the mechanisms of neurotransmitter and hormone action – the chemicals that are responsible for carrying messages between cells. And the research they're doing now is going in exactly the direction I see as the future in that particular field.'

The moment we finished our meal, he drew me over to the settee and showed me a sheaf of pamphlets he'd brought home.

'You see, most drugs act upon the transmitters and hormones which allow one cell to talk to another . . . ' he said, sketching a simple diagram in an attempt to explain the nature of his interest, ' . . . or on receptors which sense the presence of these chemicals and are present on the outside of every cell. Here.' He pointed the pencil to demonstrate. 'I'd be involved in research into what happens *inside* the cells. The biochemical machinery which makes a cell respond or change its behaviour.'

'Sounds fascinating.' I didn't understand much of his scientific jargon but I couldn't help but be caught up in his infectious excitement. 'What's the salary like?'

'Brilliant!' He mentioned what seemed an astronomical sum.

'Phil! That's a huge increase!'

He nodded.

'A new life . . . ' I said. 'In a new country.'

'It's not in the bag. There'll be other applicants . . . '

'We'd have to learn French. At least – brush up on it. I've gotten rusty since university . . . '

'Calm down, Boss!' Phil grinned. He put an arm round my shoulder and pulled me to him. 'I haven't got the job yet.'

'Oh! If only . . . How long before you'll know?'

'A fortnight, at least. They're still interviewing.'

'Oh, Phil . . . '

'Rita Gloor – Head of Personnel – said she'd be in touch.'

'If you do get it, when would we go?'

He shrugged and tempered his excitement. 'No good getting too carried away, Boss. Nothing may come of it.'

'No,' I said, slowly. 'But I have a feeling that God has a plan for us to go.'

*   *   *

We rang our respective parents and gave them the news. Sleep was impossible that night and conversation from there on in was punctuated with exclamations of 'what if . . . ?' or 'if only . . . '

The Monday following Phil's interview was August Bank Holiday and, in keeping with our traditions, we bundled Tash in the back of the car and set off for a family excursion, heading off towards Gloucestershire and the Cotswolds. The steam railway at Toddington had long been a source of attraction and certainly warranted a ride before we drove on to Tewkesbury, where we stopped and enjoyed a few hours wandering in the lovely old town, followed by tea at Bourton-on-the-Water – one of my favourite Cotswold towns. We returned home tired but happy.

Phil had the following day off and I made an early start with the housework to get it out of the way before he and Natasha awoke. No sooner had I begun, however, than the telephone rang. Clear as a bell, a foreign voice asked to speak to Dr Philip Godfrey.

My heart hammered on my ribs and I gabbled my response, then flew from the dining-room and up the stairs to rouse Phil.

'It's them! Glaxo. Rita – whatever.'

Phil ran barefoot down the stairs and grabbed the receiver. As he listened, a look of incredulity spread, slowly, across his face.

'I . . . well . . . I don't know,' he stuttered.

Then he lapsed into silence and his eyes glazed as he listened again. Finally, he said, hedgingly, 'I . . . I don't quite know what to say . . . Could I . . . could I have a think about it and let you know?'

'Quit stalling,' I mouthed. 'They might take someone else.'

He flapped a hand at me and nodded to the receiver, promising a decision when he'd had time to think. Then he hung up.

For a moment he stood stock still, stunned by the news he had heard. Then as I descended the staircase, he turned to me and said, in a shocked voice, 'They want me. For some reason they actually want me.'

'Gee, that's great . . . '

'The job's mine, if I'm willing to take it. They made that quite clear. They've given me two weeks to think about it.'

With great excitement, we discussed the pros and cons.

As the day wore on, however, Phil's initial euphoria began to wane and it became increasingly obvious that he was extremely nervous. Beneath a very natural enthusiasm, was a very real anxiety.

'What's the matter, Boss?' I asked, after a prolonged silence.

'I feel that I need to talk to various people about the health risks,' he said. 'After all, Glaxo have no idea that I have AIDS. Supposing I can't get the medical treatment I need?'

Although Phil had acquainted the Interview Board with the fact that he had haemophilia, we had decided, before he went, that he would be better not mentioning the AIDS problem.

'We'll cross that bridge when we get to it,' he'd said.

Now, here we were, almost at that point.

'I told Glaxo that Factor VIII is the most expensive of all my medication,' Phil said, 'and they're checking with their insurance company to find out if it would be covered. I think I'd better have a word with Dr Rizza.'

Together, we went down to the Haemophilia Centre, explained the situation and asked the doctor's advice.

Attentively, his arm hooked round the back of his chair, he listened to our doubts and fears, sometimes nodding and occasionally throwing in the odd question.

Finally, he straightened up and said unequivocally, 'Go for it!'

For a moment we were lost for words. This was exactly what we'd wanted to hear but somehow, it was a shock to receive approval without prevarication.

Phil summed up his feelings: 'I think I'd like to know as much as possible about the medical angle before I make any final decision.'

Dr Rizza said he would get in touch with a colleague in Geneva and also suggested that we speak with Dr Peto of Infectious Diseases. When all that was done and we had returned home, we prayed that God would show us His will.

'If He wants us to go, He'll open the doors,' I said to Phil.

That very day, Rita Gloor telephoned to say that Phil's Factor VIII would be covered by insurance and, with that confirmed, we went to see Phil's parents in Sevenoaks. They were wholeheartedly in favour of his accepting, and when I drove Phil over to Ross-on-Wye, where he had a conference to attend, we had all but made up our minds. During a trip to London, a few days later, we bought a tourist guide on Geneva and celebrated with dinner at a Mexican restaurant in Leicester Square and a visit to the National Film Theatre – where Phil was a member – to see Walt Disney's *Fantasia*. When we returned to Sevenoaks late that night, I thought how nice it was to have had a 'date'.

By 12th September, when the fortnight's grace allowed by Glaxo was up, we had reached a decision. Our intuition said Yes; Phil's doctors backed us; and most of our friends supported our aims. It seemed that God had, indeed, opened all the right doors.

'I rang Glaxo from Steve Watson's lab, to tell them I'd accept the job,' Phil said when he returned from work that day. His boss, Professor David Graham-Smith, had congratulated him warmly, he told me. However, it all seemed too much for Phil. He spent the evening feeling shattered.

Not so me. The very next day, I bought two folders. One for 'Leaving Oxford'. And the other, 'Moving to Geneva'.

5

Moving Mountains

'Fear not, for I have redeemed you, I have called you by name; you are mine. When you pass through the waters, I will be with you, and when you pass through the rivers, they will not sweep over you.'

Isaiah 43:1–3

No matter how often I flew, the power and thrust of the modern jet engine never failed to excite me. On that dreary November morning when we'd been waiting, earlier, in Gatwick's departure lounge for our British Airways flight to Geneva, I'd found myself reflecting: an aircraft was so huge and cumbersome a machine that, had experience not shown me otherwise, the thought of its ever being able to leave the ground and soar into the sky would have defied my imagination. Yet now that we were airborne, other aircraft and the terminal buildings that had appeared so dominant at ground level, had retreated into insignificant proportions, far beneath us.

Just so, are God's promises. We know from the Bible that He is 'able to do immeasurably more than all we ask or imagine, according to His power that is at work within us'. To 'know' in theory, however, is not to 'know' in practice. To Phil and to me, there might sometimes have appeared to be little evidence of that promise in recent years: adversity had loomed large in our lives; Phil's body was being systematically destroyed by AIDS; our material life was one of comparative penury; and there had seemed no hope for the future.

Yet experience had shown that God is able. He had not taken us out of our circumstances and healed Phil of his illness. What He had done was to demonstrate that if we were obedient to Him, His power would be at work within us, lifting us above all that threatened to keep us earthbound, to soar on wings like eagles.

The No Smoking signs went off and I settled back in my seat and looked through the porthole. The 757 had been climbing steadily through a dense layer of murky cloud. Suddenly, we emerged into dazzling sunshine. And seen from this side, the grey clouds were a sea of billowing white cumulus, rimmed with gold.

I squeezed Phil's hand. 'Isn't it wonderful the way God works things out?'

'You mean this trip?' He put down his book and considered the matter.

'That too,' I answered. 'But I was thinking more of the Arkinstalls. Imagine! Of all people, they turn out to be Christians too.'

Steve Arkinstall had called Phil up on the phone one day at work, about a month after Phil had accepted the job with Glaxo.

'I'm ringing to introduce myself,' Steve had explained. 'I'm about to take up a position in Geneva, with Glaxo, and I understand that we'll be working together in the same department.'

Phil had told me of their conversation when he'd returned home that evening. 'He sounded like a great guy. I couldn't believe it when he told me that Glaxo had received ninety-eight applications for my job! Apparently, they only interviewed five. All foreigners. Steve said he'd been told that I was the top candidate.'

''Course you were!' I'd replied, unequivocally. 'Is he married?'

'Simonne – I think that's what his wife's called. Sounds

rather French, doesn't it? They've got a daughter, too, called Emilie. Would you like to meet them? Steve's invited the three of us for dinner. They live in Long Hanborough.'

We'd driven over one Friday evening in October. The moment we'd arrived I'd noticed a Sunday School sheet of Emilie's on the hall table, and over dinner had discovered that the Arkinstalls were Christians. Steve was as young and boyish looking as Phil, with a similar taste in humour and music and it was evident, right from the start, that the two hit it off well together. Simonne, dark and pretty, was indeed part French – on her mother's side – with a capable and vivacious air about her that almost took your breath away. Her transparent and self-effacing honesty, coupled with a brisk, matter-of-fact manner, made her an easy confidante. I felt sure that even had we not found a mutuality of faith, the four of us would have become firm friends; with Steve and Simonne's enthusiastic espousal of Christian truths, however, there was no doubt. Our friendship was clinched.

A stewardess approached with refreshments and I let down the tray in front of me. When we had been served, I turned again to Phil.

'Doesn't it make you feel that God has a plan for us?' I asked. 'This job. Steve and Simonne. It can't just be coincidence.'

Phil picked at the food in front of him. 'I still feel slightly worried about the whole business of going abroad to live,' he admitted. 'Well, more nervous than worried, I suppose.' He paused, then turned to me and grinned. 'But what hope have I got with you driving me on?'

He waited, obviously hoping that I would rise to the bait, but I was well used to his teasing and after a moment he grew more sober. 'No. Seriously. It's your excitement and enthusiasm that give me heart. I'm sure you're right. Whatever happens, we're in the Lord's hands.'

Satisfied with his response, I returned his grin, then removed the packaging from my in-flight meal and tucked in heartily.

*   *   *

From Geneva airport we took a taxi to Glaxo and I was afforded my first sight of the famous Lac Léman though, disappointingly, the *jet d'eau* was not in evidence. The huge water spout which, so my guide book told me, shot out of the lake to a height of a hundred and forty metres (more than 450 feet) apparently did not operate in the winter months. However, the city of Geneva met all my expectations. Bounding both sides of the southernmost tip of the lake, it extended some miles along the banks of the rivers Rhône and Arve. The north shore of the lake was dominated by hotels and offices of gracious Georgian-like proportions, which displayed, in neon lights – though in an entirely ungarish manner – the source of the city's wealth: famous names in watchmaking, jewellery, industry and banking. Amongst the hotels, Phil showed me La Paix, where Glaxo had put him up on his previous trip.

'The city's surrounded on three sides by France,' he told me. 'And that mountain you see over there is La Salève. They say the view from the top is superb.'

I couldn't help but be impressed. The streets were clean and bright; boats bobbed on the ruffled waters of the lake; and in the twilight the city sparkled like a faceted gemstone in a setting of distant, snow-sprinkled mountains.

We were met at the Glaxo offices by Rita Gloor, Head of Personnel, and Véronique Stofer, her assistant. Rita was a woman of immense capability and calm, some years older than Phil and me. She had the French flair for understated chic, and her hair was a glossy auburn cap that lay close to her head in a jaw-length bob. Her command of English was excellent, though heavily overlayed with a Swiss-French accent and, together with Véronique, she could not have been more welcoming.

'So good to see you again, Phil.' She shook his hand warmly then turned to me. 'And you must be Phil's wife? He has spoken of you. You don't mind if I call you Jana?'

Rita pronounced my name with a hard 'a' as in Jane – a change from the long 'a' with which I was usually addressed, and which rendered it 'Jahna'. Few people, reading it for the first time rather than hearing it, seemed to hit on the correct pronunciation: Jana as in manna.

'You have a little daughter?' she asked as she showed us through the foyer where, appropriately, a Swiss cheese plant and a huge free-form clock were displayed.

'Natasha. But she's back home with her grandma in Sevenoaks.' I stepped into the lift indicated by Véronique, closely followed by Phil and Rita Gloor.

Once in the office, we were given an itinerary of flats to view.

'We have made appointments for you to see all these tomorrow,' Rita said, running a pencil down the list. 'And these are for the following day.' She turned the page.

We learned that the legislation governing property ownership in Switzerland was strictly observed. Foreigners living and working in the country may purchase housing only after a qualification period of residence – usually five to ten years. Even then, phenomenally high land prices made home ownership prohibitive and we would, therefore, be expected to rent accommodation for the duration of Phil's contract with Glaxo. This suited us fine because we could then keep on the house in Percy Street and lease it out.

Rita gave us a bundle of maps and guide books – which included David Hampshire's *Survival Handbook*, a copy of which I had bought in London – then handed us over to Véronique.

'She will take you to your accommodation,' Rita said.

We were to be put up at Glaxo's expense in an apartment owned by them in the Résidence Dalphin, which was centrally situated in a quarter called Carouge. As soon as we were installed, we unpacked then went out for dinner.

Next morning, guided by Catherine – one of the Glaxo secretaries – we set off, armed with the list of appointments and, amongst the many apartments that we viewed, found one that we really liked. That afternoon we met up with Steve and Simonne, who joined us in flat-hunting and later for dinner in the company's studio apartment.

'What have you seen so far?' Simonne asked as soon as they arrived.

I showed her the list. 'We saw one this morning that we both loved. It was so pretty – looked just as you imagine a Swiss house, with a steep roof and a balcony outside where you could grow things . . . .'

'I love gardening,' said Simonne. 'And I'd like to have somewhere for Emilie to play. How big is this place you've seen?'

'Bigger than our house in Oxford,' I replied. 'We both like it. And it's not far out of town.'

Switzerland was divided into *cantons* – the equivalent of English shires, except that each was autonomous – and these were subdivided into districts called *communes*. The flat that we liked was in the Chêne-Bourg *commune* which, according to the map, was south of the lake, a mere twenty-minute tram ride from the *centre-ville*. Next morning, after completing our viewing schedule, Catherine took us to the estate agent.

'It's the flat in rue du Gothard that we're interested in,' Phil told her.

Catherine translated for us and filled in forms on our behalf.

'Gee,' I said, when we came out of the agent's office, 'now that we've got an address, it makes the move seem so much more real!'

Back at the Glaxo office, however, we discovered that things were not quite that straightforward. Rita Gloor listened patiently to our enthusiasm regarding our 'new home', then gently put us right.

'Don't get your hopes up too high or you may be disappointed,' she said. 'Demand for good flats outstrips supply. It's just possible that the *régie* might turn down your request.'

But our excitement was not so easily to be doused.

'The next thing is to open up a bank account,' Rita reminded us and again Catherine accompanied us to help.

'Pretty nifty,' said Phil when we emerged later into bright sunshine. 'Never thought I'd have a "Swiss bank account".'

We bade Catherine goodbye, then Phil studied the guide book that Rita had given him.

'Where now?' he asked. And like two big kids on a school outing, we set off in search of a tea room.

'Don't you get the feeling, more and more, that God is leading us on?' I asked, as we waited to cross the broad main street in Geneva's area of commerce.

Phil grinned. 'Definitely!' And he grabbed my hand as we dodged the traffic and negotiated our way to the other side.

*   *   *

We spent the next few days sightseeing and shopping in the company of the Arkinstalls.

'It's Remembrance Day tomorrow,' Steve reminded us as we parted on Saturday evening. 'Simonne and I thought we'd go to the Anglican church, Holy Trinity. Shall we see you there?'

Next day, after the service, the four of us agreed that the 'high' church atmosphere had not been entirely to our liking and that we had better make enquiries as to a fellowship more suited to our spiritual needs.

'Don't worry,' Steve said. 'Simonne's got a contact. The friend of a friend. We'll get all the gen and keep you informed.'

Phil's dad was in Geneva on business so, after lunching

in France with the Arkinstalls, we dined with him that night.

'I can't wait to move out here,' I confided to him. 'I just love the food!'

Dad had good news for us of Phil's sister's family. We had known before we left home that Paulette had been safely delivered of a baby boy but that haemophilia had been diagnosed. What we didn't know, was the result of further tests that had been made.

'You'll be pleased to hear,' Dad told us, 'that according to initial findings, Jonathan David is in the clear. There are no signs of the SCIDS that caused James' death.'

'Thank God!' Phil was particularly glad. He and Paulette had been close since childhood and I suspected that, as a haemophiliac himself, they had been drawn still closer through the shared adversity.

'That's wonderful,' I agreed. And I was convinced that this was one more evidence of God's goodness and love.

*   *   *

Our flight home on the Monday was uneventful and, *en route* for Oxford, we stopped off at Ikea, north of London, to buy dishes and a dining-table for the future tenants of Percy Street. Next day, I began telephoning removal companies.

'The move seems more and more real,' I said to Phil.

Then two days later, disaster struck. I woke on the morning of 14th November to find that Natasha was not well.

'I've left her in bed,' I said to Phil over breakfast. 'She's right off her food and she's got the runs.'

He looked up from buttering his toast and said, with concern, 'It's probably this gastroenteritis that's doing the rounds.'

'Well it couldn't have happened at a worse time,' I retorted. 'The builders are coming this morning to put in the new windows and doors.'

The agents who were to deal with leasing our house had told us, when they'd inspected the property, that the frames of both front windows, upstairs and down, and the front door itself, were rotten and needed to be replaced. It would be cold and draughty whilst the job was being executed; however, I dared not put it off.

'You know what builders are like,' I said.

'I wasn't thinking about that so much . . . ' Phil replied, quietly, but when I shot a look at him he refused to be drawn and, after a moment, he left the table and went upstairs. From his footfall overhead, I knew that he had gone to see Tash, and when he left for work a few moments later, I thought nothing of it.

*   *   *

Within two days Phil was suffering similar symptoms to Natasha's, and by Thanksgiving – when I did a special dinner for Mum and Dad, who were visiting – there was no doubt that he had gastroenteritis.

'He's spent the whole day in bed, or trotting off to the toilet,' I said to Mum, when I'd taken her coat and she and Dad had settled in the living-room.

'Has the doctor been?' she asked.

'No. You know Phil. He never wants to bother him if he thinks it's nothing out of the ordinary.'

'Shall I go up and see if he's well enough to eat with us?' she asked, persuasively.

I knew that if anyone could get Phil to rally it would be Mum but, to my surprise, she was unsuccessful. Whilst we tucked in to roast turkey and all the trimmings, he languished, sick and feverish, in bed.

When we'd washed up, I took Phil a fresh jug of water. He looked pale and thin, alone in the wide expanse of our double bed. I removed a dirty glass from the floor, filled a clean one and set it beside him. He lay watching me, his eyes half-closed.

'I'm scared I'm going to be really ill and not be

able to take up my appointment with Glaxo,' he said, quietly.

I picked up his trousers from where they had fallen, then perched on the edge of the bed. 'You'll be okay, honey.' With an effort, I injected my voice with more optimism than I felt.

'I'm not so sure,' he replied. 'One of the things about this disease is that you pick up everything that's going. I feel really depressed about the possibilities.'

In the corner of the room, the TV programme that Phil had been watching came to an end. The flickering shadows on the screen cvoked a ghostly pallor in Phil's face.

He said, 'I feel really grotty.'

My heart sank. There was nothing more swiftly debilitating than diarrhoea. Given his condition, he didn't need to spell out the implications. We were due in Geneva in the New Year and this was 19th November. Those six weeks or so could make or break us.

*   *   *

'Well, there appear to be no bugs in your samples, according to this.'

Dr Peto looked up from the report he had been studying. His face was grave. As the Consultant Physician of Infectious Diseases to whom Phil had been referred after his attack of pneumocystis, he was fully *au fait* with the gravity of Phil's case. A brown-haired man of medium build, he had a slightly rumpled appearance that made him eminently approachable. Nevertheless, on the other side of the desk, Phil shifted uncomfortably on the hard plastic chair on which he was seated. He sighed.

'I had hoped they'd have found something.'

Dr Peto nodded in sympathy. 'It would have made treatment easier.'

'So what happens now?' Disappointment was etched in Phil's face, darkening his eyes and wiping the usual smile from his mouth.

Regretfully, Dr Peto closed the file on his desk. Then he looked up and said, kindly but frankly, 'I don't know that there's much we can do at the moment, Dr Godfrey. We've run all the tests that are pertinent. And the lab report seems to cover everything . . . '

'So it's just "Keep taking the tablets",' Phil said, in an attempt to crack a joke, but the tension in his body was evident as he gripped the sides of the chair.

'I'm afraid so,' Dr Peto said, helplessly. 'The usual thing . . . Immodium. Plenty of fluids to make sure you don't get dehydrated . . . You know the routine.'

Rigid with disappointment, Phil rose to his feet, shook the doctor's hand, and turned to leave the room. With the briefest of smiles, I followed him out.

*   *   *

Phil's condition had worsened in the two days following the Thanksgiving dinner I had prepared for Mum and Dad's visit, and I had taken him into the John Warin Ward at the Churchill Hospital, where he had undergone a series of tests. The lack of result was worrying. Preparations for our impending departure for Geneva were proceeding apace. Replacement of the windows and door of number seventy-three was now complete, requiring only my attention with a paintbrush to be ready for our tenants. Then we had learned, to our delight, that the flat in Chêne-Bourg was ours. Everything seemed to be coming together for our move – except for Phil's continuing poor health.

'I'm really scared that I'm not going to be well enough in time for us to go,' he said, crawling between bed and toilet. It was tough going, as our room was upstairs in the front, and the lavatory was at the back of the terrace on the ground floor.

'Yes, you will,' I said determinedly. 'Tash is better now. And besides, there's over a month before we leave.'

Nevertheless, I was grateful when Mum and Dad prayed with us before they left for home.

Two days later, Phil had additional problems.

'There's blood in my stools,' he said. 'I think you'd better take me down to the Haemophilia Centre, Jana.'

Whatever next, Lord? I cried silently.

The loss of blood had rendered Phil severely anaemic, so Dr Rizza arranged for him to have a blood transfusion at the hospital the following day.

Phil's concern was apparent. 'I've so much work to finish at the lab before I leave,' he said in despair, when I took him back to the Churchill next day.

'You'll cope.' I parked the car and locked up.

Hesitantly, Phil admitted to his real fears. 'I'm just not at all sure about this new job . . . ' he said. 'I'm afraid I won't be up to the move. I keep asking God if we're doing the right thing.'

I paused in the act of taking his overnight bag from the boot of the car and turned to look at him. 'Honey, we've prayed all along for God's guidance and your parents have prayed for your health . . . Have faith!'

'But there's so much to do. How can I organise everything if I'm stuck in hospital?'

I took Phil's arm. His sense of frustration was understandable – even commendable – but one of my strengths was my organisational ability. Not for nothing had I worked as a bus tour co-ordinator!

'If that's all you're worrying about . . . ' I said cheerfully.

And together we proceeded to Admissions.

*   *   *

The next few weeks were difficult. Christmas was coming up; Tash had to be kept occupied; and there was the sorting and packing to be done before our departure for Geneva. In addition, Phil's diarrhoea showed no signs of abating and, with him in and out of hospital for transfusions, it fell to me to show prospective tenants around the house and to liaise with agencies.

We had decided to lease the house for six months initially, so that if things didn't work out in Geneva – given Phil's state of health – we had a bolt hole to return to. Moreover, Phil had arranged a further safety net at work.

'I've talked it through with Prof and he's made a brilliant suggestion,' Phil told me one day when he returned from the lab. 'Officially, I shall be taking a sort of "leave of absence". That means that if we have to come home, I've still got a job to come back to.'

In silence, I wrestled with my feelings. Then continuing with my task of laying the table for dinner, I asked tentatively, 'I wonder if making all these contingency plans shows that we're not really trusting God?'

Phil sat down at the half-laid table. 'Jana,' he said earnestly, 'believe me, I want to go to Geneva as much as you do. But you and Tash are my responsibility. It wouldn't be honouring to God if I reneged on that responsibility now would it?'

I sat down and faced him. 'But if we believe that He's taking us to Switzerland, surely we must believe He can keep us there?'

'Are you absolutely certain that it's His will?'

'Yes.'

'But for what purpose? Do you know why God is taking us there?'

In all honesty, I couldn't answer that. But I knew that if we continued to listen to God, He would lead us and guide us.

Phil hunched over the table and, supporting his head in his hands, he closed his eyes and pressed his fingers into the lids. When he opened them, he said, 'Trusting God, as I see it, is about pushing doors to see if they'll open. It would be foolish to rush into things without thought. We still don't know if I can get health insurance in Switzerland. Boss, we've just got to take things one step at a time.'

Dubiously, I surveyed him. And after a moment, a lopsided grin appeared on his face.

'Honestly, Jana! If I had my way, we wouldn't be going at all. It's only your faith that encourages me to think that there might be a reason . . . '

He reached across the table and took my hand. And with that, I had to be satisfied.

*   *   *

On 6th December, after purchasing our flight tickets for Geneva, I took Phil into hospital for a further transfusion and biopsy. Next morning, Mum came over to keep me company for the day, whilst the removal company packed up our belongings. Natasha had a great time playing with the tape with which the men sealed the packing cases, though she cried when she saw her toybox being carried out of the door. I collected Phil from hospital that afternoon.

Towards the end of the week, he again found that he had blood in his stools.

'It's bad!' he said simply.

I rang Mum and arranged for her to have Natasha to stay until we joined the family in Sevenoaks for Christmas. Then I took Phil to the hospital, where Dr Peto examined him.

'You've been taking your concern over this move too hard,' he said. 'I think we'd better keep you in again for observation.'

The following day, I took Tash to Mum's. I was full of nervous energy and tackled every task with gusto, arranging to have an accountant look after our income from the house and the tax that this would incur, cancelling direct debits with the bank, sending out notification of our change of address. Finally, with the help of our fellowship group, I undertook some necessary redecorating of the living-room and dining-room.

We had given up leadership of the group when Phil had accepted the job at Glaxo, and Richard Mason had taken over. He and his wife, Hilary, had been good friends to us and were sad to see us go. At their behest, the group threw a farewell-cum-Christmas party for us – in the form of a Chinese feast from the local take-away. Phil was released temporarily from hospital for the occasion, and we were presented with gifts – a hardback music version of *Songs and Hymns of Fellowship* and a video of the horror movie *Robocop*. Next day, we attended a similar event at the lab – though rather upmarket in that we had champagne and cakes – and Phil was given a book and a watercolour of Oxford. That afternoon we heard from the agent that a young couple had just signed an agreement for tenancy of 73 Percy Street, for the next six months.

When I next visited Phil in hospital, he told me that Dr Peto had asked to see me before I took him home on 21st December. Accordingly, I went first to the doctor's office in the John Radcliffe Hospital. It was a large room, comfortably furnished with an upholstered settee, and when I had seated myself, the doctor sat beside me, half-turned in my direction.

'How are you feeling about the move?' he began.

'Well,' I folded my hands in my lap, wondering what was coming. 'I'm a bit worried, but I still want to go.'

Dr Peto nodded. 'I asked you to come in to see me so that we could talk through some of the ramifications. You understand that Phil's treatment in Switzerland may be quite different to the way we do things here?'

'Oh?'

Dr Peto explained. 'We try to let the body develop its own natural resources to cope with each illness. You may find that the doctors in Switzerland are more inclined to experiment with drugs and alternative treatments.' He smiled, reassuringly. 'I wanted you to be aware of this possibility. And to let you know that I'm always available; you have only to pick up the phone if you have any concerns.'

Gratefully, I acknowledged his kindness. Then I said, 'Phil told me that he'd asked you what the end would be like. He said you'd told him that he would feel worse and worse, and gradually his body would give up.'

Suddenly, without warning, I broke down. Tears streamed down my cheeks, and as I leaned forward to hide my face in my hands, my shoulders began to heave. Dr Peto moved closer, slipped a comforting arm around me, and passed me a tissue from a box which was to hand.

'Thank you,' I sniffed.

As my sobs abated, the doctor removed his arm and I sat back. 'I don't think I could have coped with all of this if I didn't believe that God is in control,' I said. Then I shot him a watery glance. 'Are you a Christian?'

It was the first time I had felt able to talk openly of my faith with anyone outside our circle of family and friends, and vaguely I wondered if my tears had brought about this release.

Dr Peto smiled, wryly. Then he said, 'I'm not sure I know how to answer that. I suppose you could call me confused . . . '

*   *   *

We drove down to Sevenoaks on 22nd December. That evening Phil threw up his dinner and had a temperature which kept him in bed throughout the following day. By the time the Maxteds arrived on Christmas Eve, Phil was evidently feeling emotionally overwhelmed. However, he seemed to rally after a long talk with David and, though nothing was said to me, I guessed that he felt reassured to know that, in his brother-in-law, he was in good medical care. Whilst the rest of the family went to church, David helped Phil with his treatment.

Dr Peto had given instructions prior to Phil's release from hospital. A needle, inserted into a vein in the back of Phil's hand, had been strapped in place so that a drip could be set up at home to administer his medication. David removed the clip from the end of the tube and checked that the flow was bubble-free. Swiftly, he inserted the tube into the apparatus on Phil's wrist, then opened the valve so that the drip could pass through the needle.

Phil slept badly and woke early on Christmas morning, so I used that as an excuse to open our stockings at 5 a.m. I had had to buy most of the presents he gave me, but he'd had Mum get a few surprises. By breakfast time, when Natasha was confronted with her pile of gifts from beneath the tree, Phil appeared faintly bemused.

'Are you feeling okay and enjoying everything, honey?' I asked, but it was evident that much of the day's events had passed him by and he was more than happy to stay in bed whilst we went to church.

On the way home, David and I stopped off at Sevenoaks hospital to pick up some more equipment for Phil. As soon as we got in, David hooked up the amphiteracyn drip to Phil's arm; and the acyclovir, which was an antiviral drug that the doctors in Oxford had given him in the hopes of combating the diarrhoea.

Later, I popped in to the bedroom to see how he was doing.

'I can't remember David setting all this up,' he confessed, weakly. 'I feel so unwell . . . '

On another occasion, much to my alarm, he admitted to having pins and needles in his feet.

Then, in a more lucid moment, he said, 'I feel awful knowing that you're doing all the work, organising the move, while I'm doing nothing.'

My heart went out to him. 'You just use all your strength to get well again.'

The day after Boxing Day, David and Paulette left for home with their boys and, soon after their departure, we returned to Oxford where Phil was due for more tests at the Churchill Hospital. As soon as I had made arrangements to pick him up next day, I set off for Percy Street, in order to tie up various loose ends. That night was the last that I spent in our house.

Sadness impinged upon my excitement when we left Oxford next morning. Who knew if and when we would return? Back at Sevenoaks, however, the question raised by the remainder of the family was whether we should be leaving for Geneva at all?

'I'm terribly worried,' Mum said when Natasha was in bed and we had all congregated in the kitchen. 'I just don't see how you'll make it with Phil in his present condition.'

Dad agreed. 'You'll be a long way from home. Of course we'll help all we can. But even in an emergency, it would be a while before we could get over there.'

'Do think carefully,' Mum urged us. 'What does Dr Rizza have to say?'

Outside, in the carport adjacent to the kitchen, the wind soughed fretfully, jerking at the curtains at the window. My nerves jangled in response and I gripped the worktop edge, against which I leaned. The stresses of recent weeks were taking their toll. In the front room, where we'd left him, Phil lay on the settee, obviously exhausted. It didn't feel right to be discussing him in his absence. I looked down at my feet, then at Mum.

'He gave Phil a letter in case we have to postpone our trip. Just to say that he's not well enough to travel . . . '

Although I could understand the concern of Phil's family, I was unhappy with the way things were developing.

Later, when we were in bed in the privacy of our own room, I shared my feelings with Phil. His response was disappointing.

'I hate to say it, but I think they're right,' he said. 'I'm really beginning to have my doubts about the wisdom of the whole venture.'

Wind shook the windowpane and an icy draught sliced down the middle of the bed. Tucking the duvet under my chin, I pulled up my knees and huddled down in search of warmth.

'I'm sure God means us to go,' I insisted. 'After all, He's brought us so far . . . '

Beside me, Phil lay inert and silent. After a moment, he sighed.

'I just don't know any more, Jana. Perhaps this latest illness is a sign that we're not meant to . . . '

'I know it seems that way, honey. And I admit that I don't know what He means for us to do once we get there. But He hasn't closed the door and I can't believe He wants us to go backwards. You'll be well again . . . '

Fervently, I hoped that I was right.

But if I took heart when Phil accompanied me to church – for the first time since our return from Geneva – on the morning of New Year's Eve, my optimism was short lived. By the time we boarded our flight at Gatwick on the morning of 3rd January, 1990, bound for our new life in Geneva, I was as worried as anyone. I hid it well.

6

Mountains are for Climbing

'He who dwells in the shelter of the Most High will rest in the shadow of the Almighty. I will say of the Lord, "He is my refuge and my fortress, my God in whom I trust".'

Psalm 91:1–2

Although our furniture and effects had arrived from England in December, we initially took up residence in another of Glaxo's furnished flats at the Résidence Dalphin. Phil's appearance, as I happily unpacked our stuff, was that of a man who barely knew what was going on. Indeed, one night, in search of a drink of water, he took the wrong bottle from the fridge and ended up with a mouthful of salad dressing! In addition, he was suffering considerable pain in his feet.

Swiss regulations demanded that all new residents have a chest X-ray at the hospital, and Glaxo had made appropriate arrangements for Phil to attend. As soon as he left, I made up my mind to make an appointment for him to have a check-up. Dr Rizza had alerted the haemophilia department in the Hôpital Cantonal as to Phil's medical needs, and had sent us a copy of their response. I dialled the telephone number shown on the letterhead, explained the situation in halting French, and was delighted to be given a time that afternoon.

Shortly before noon, Simonne came by with her four-year-old daughter, Emilie.

'You seem to be settling in well,' she said, evidently astonished with the progress I had made. 'You're so well organised, Jana.'

With a degree of pride, I admitted that bringing order out of chaos was an important aspect of my life. Then I thought of the disease that was wreaking havoc in Phil's body. In the face of that 'disorder' – which was so totally alien to the harmony of God's creation – I was helpless.

'I haven't finished unpacking properly yet,' Simonne admitted, accepting the coffee I had made. Then she grinned. 'Still . . . doesn't matter. Things are going to be pretty chaotic in our household for a while, I shouldn't wonder.'

Her remark hinted at some exciting secret that was bursting to be revealed. I looked up quickly.

'Oh? Why's that?' I enquired, ingenuously.

With unsuppressed glee, Simonne replied: 'Because I'm pregnant.'

I felt the smile freeze on my face. The open hearth in one corner of the room looked cheerless and cold, and suddenly all my attempts at creating a home – albeit a temporary one – took on an empty insignificance.

Clearly concerned by my reaction, Simonne frowned. 'Are you okay?'

There was no way that she could have known . . . I swallowed, composed my features with care and nodded.

It was obvious that she was not convinced. 'What is it? What have I said?' she cried.

I stood up and, on the pretext of taking my mug out to the kitchen, turned my back on her.

'I'm really pleased for you,' I said over my shoulder.

That, at least, was true.

Simonne, however, was not so easily to be fobbed off and followed me out of the room. She put a hand on my shoulder and spoke softly. 'Have I said the wrong thing, Jana?'

Her sensitivity was disarming; and returning to the sitting-room, I found myself telling her the whole sorry story.

'I really am pleased for you,' I said again. 'But . . . well . . . it's just that I'd love another baby . . . '

Simonne sat opposite me. Her eyes never left my face as she waited for me to go on. Part of me wished I had never begun. Would a revelation of Phil's condition jeopardise our friendship with the Arkinstalls? Or was that friendship a part of God's plan – one of the reasons, perhaps, in some small way, for which we'd been brought to Geneva?

My hands shook. I pressed them down between my thighs. Then tense with anxiety, I said quietly, 'Phil has AIDS.'

Simonne sat, stunned. I thought I had blown it, and my heart hammered, wildly. Somewhere – in another part of the building – a door slammed. The sound echoed emptily in my mind.

Then Simonne reached out; covered my hand with her own. Her eyes were enormous, brimming with tears. For a moment she seemed at a loss.

Then she whispered, 'Oh, Jana . . . '

* * *

With characteristic kindness, Simonne offered transport when it was time to collect Phil from his medical, and insisted that she would look after Natasha for the remainder of the afternoon, so that I was free. Shortly before we left home, Phil rang to say that he had returned from the hospital to Rita Gloor's office at Glaxo.

'Okay, we'll pick you up from there,' I said. 'You've got an appointment with a Dr Vogel at the haematology department at three.'

'Fine.'

The line crackled.

'Have you told them at Glaxo about your condition?' I

asked, unaware that Rita was within earshot. Phil replied guardedly.

Later, when Simonne drove me over to collect him, I learned why.

'It must have been obvious to Rita from my conversation with you that something was going on,' he said, climbing into the front passenger seat. 'I felt I had no option but to break the news. She took it very well. In fact, she was very sympathetic.'

Simonne deposited Phil and me at the hospital, where we had a good chat with Dr Vogel. Fortunately, he spoke English well, because we had some difficulty in convincing him that, since we had no medical insurance as yet, keeping Phil in would not be a wise move. We would never have managed to explain in French!

Throughout the next day, Phil continued to be withdrawn. And when I took him over to the flat in Chêne-Bourg, where Steve and Simonne had promised to help rig up some lights for us, he took little pleasure in their company.

Next day, whilst Phil stayed at home, the Arkinstalls took Natasha and me to the Evangelical Baptist Church of Geneva. From the outside, the church was an unprepossessing building in a somewhat grubby terrace in the old quarter of Geneva. Once through the gateway, however, a pretty cobbled courtyard was revealed, with schoolrooms on one side and the sanctuary on the other.

I looked around me with interest, as we entered the church. Cord matting covered much of the uneven stone-flagged floor, upon which rows of wooden chairs were set before a raised altar. The walls were plain and unadorned, relieved only by the effects of a shallow domed roof and skylights, through which the winter sun was softly diffused.

Before the service began, Steve introduced me to the pastor, Derek Adamsbaum, and his wife Beryl, both of whom lived in France. I guessed them to be in their fifties. Derek, tall and with a receding hairline, turned out to be

an impassioned preacher, while Beryl, petite and dark
haired, was, I soon learned, a gifted Bible teacher. Then
Steve filled me in on some of the 'gen' he'd gleaned as
promised.

The church had been started twenty-one years previously by Francis Schaeffer, founder of the Swiss retreat,
L'Abri. Its cosmopolitan congregation and spiritual sen-
sibility were evidence of the ongoing Life and Christ-
centredness in which it had been conceived. There was
a sense of unity that, despite a transient membership,
linked us not only with those currently worshipping at
EBCG, but with all those who had gone before. How
I wished Phil had been with me, to experience this for
himself.

His absence was cause for concern to all who greeted me
and I was greatly encouraged when prayer requests were
invited to be made known to the fellowship.

'Would you like Phil's name to be put forward?' Steve
asked, and I nodded.

At the end of the service, I fielded enquiries with a
half-truth.

'He's suffering from an acute attack of gastroenteritis,'
I explained.

The moment Steve dropped us off at the apartment, I
ran upstairs and went straight to the bedroom, eager to
relate the morning's events to Phil.

'I'm sure we'll be at home in no time,' I said, dropping
on to the bed. 'Everyone was so friendly.'

*   *   *

Next morning, Rita Gloor arrived at the flat with Dr
Jonathan Knowles, Director of the Institute and, therefore, Head of Glaxo in Switzerland.

He shook my hand. 'Welcome to Geneva.'

Rita smiled. 'We thought we'd leave you to settle in for
a few days before calling.'

With a good deal of trepidation, I invited them in.

Whatever would they think when they saw Phil? I called a warning.

'Guess who's come to see you, honey.'

Phil had pulled himself up from a reclining position on the sofa by the time we reached the living-room door. His face was thin and pale, tense with anxiety. We had already discussed this scenario and were terrified that with his condition now an open secret, Glaxo would ask him to leave. Nervously, he stumbled to his feet and made some attempt at a greeting when I ushered his visitors in and offered them seats.

'How are you, Phil?' Rita asked, kindly.

'Not looking too good,' said Dr Knowles.

'He's always recovered so well in the past,' I said, defensively.

As if his appearance was not bad enough, Phil seemed to be inflicted with a panicky need to explain himself. On and on he babbled.

'I don't remember much . . . The last few weeks have been a blur . . . All I recall is having a hard time making it to the toilet before being caught out . . . I seem to be having awful trouble walking . . . '

There was a terrible sense of doom as I listened to Phil digging his own pit. Eventually, I could bear it no longer. I cleared my throat.

'Phil,' I said, with acute embarrassment, 'you've done nothing but talk of the toilet, honey.'

Finally, he seemed to come to his senses and propped himself upright on the big sofa on which he was slumped.

'Jana's right. You must be wondering what's going on . . . '

Under the scrutiny of Rita and Dr Knowles, Phil's voice petered out. My heart thumped wildly. This was it! After all the waffle we were down to the nitty gritty. Now we would be sent home ignominiously . . .

'All I wondered . . . ' Dr Knowles began.

Miserably, I clenched my hands in my lap. Around me, the heavy, dark furniture of the company flat pressed in on all sides. It was typically Swiss, I thought, and wondered who had chosen it. The few pieces we'd bought from Ikea were light honey-coloured pine. Would the shop take them back if Phil were sacked?

'I only wondered,' Dr Knowles continued, 'why you didn't tell us of your condition when you came for interview in August?'

'I suppose,' Phil said with a croak, 'that I was afraid to . . .'

Dr Knowles leaned forward and rested his forearms on his knees. 'But didn't you realise that we'd have to know sooner or later? An AIDS test forms part of the medical examination for new residents.'

Phil cleared his throat. 'I thought I might not be hired,' he said. 'And I didn't want *that* to be the reason.'

For a moment – but ever so briefly – there was silence. Then Dr Knowles shook his head and sat back in his chair.

'All those who saw you at interview were of one mind,' he said firmly. 'You were seen as having a valuable contribution to make in your particular field of research.'

'I wasn't out to deceive you,' Phil said. 'You knew of my haemophilia and I suppose I thought that once I'd started work . . .'

Gently, Jonathan Knowles interrupted him. 'You'll be part of a team, Phil. And we'll support you in whatever way seems appropriate. All you need to worry about is getting well again and regaining your strength.'

I glanced at Phil. He looked as stunned and relieved as I felt. We weren't going to be thrown out after all!

'It's probably better if you say nothing of this to any of the Glaxo staff.' Rita looked to Dr Knowles for confirmation. 'I don't foresee any antipathy towards you, but I feel that your privacy should be assured.'

The director agreed. 'And you'd better take as much time as you need to convalesce.'

Phil looked suitably grateful. 'But it's not just the gastric problem,' he admitted. 'There's my legs too.'

Again, Rita answered in her capacity as Head of Personnel.

'We will do all we can to expedite insurance for your medical expenses,' she said. 'And I will speak with Dr Hirschel. He is a Consultant at l'Hôpital Cantonal and is head of the AIDS division. Yes?' Here she turned to Dr Knowles for corroboration. 'In the meantime, in the absence of cover, I would suggest that it might be better for Phil to go back to England. Perhaps the doctors there can find out what is wrong.'

Rita's summary of the situation was admirable and her suggestion eminently sensible. Clearly, it met with Dr Knowles' approval.

'Fine,' he said. And rising to his feet, he wished Phil well and indicated that it was time for him and Rita to take their leave.

Rita turned at the door on her way out.

'Get better soon,' she called. Then they were gone.

'Phew! I feel as if I sweated that one out,' Phil said to me after they had left.

'Too right!' I exclaimed. 'You did go on . . . '

'Did I? How?'

'On and on . . . There can't be too many people who start a new job by telling the managing director all the gory details of their guts.'

Phil looked mildly aghast.

'I thought you were gonna be without a job,' I said.

He grinned. 'For a moment – so did I.'

*   *   *

The following day, Phil had an appointment with a Dr Wintsch of Infectious Diseases and, a day or two later, after a blood transfusion at l'Hôpital Cantonal, arrangements were made for him to return to the UK.

'It makes sense,' he said, when he saw how worried I was. 'I'm becoming increasingly concerned about the loss of feeling in my feet. And the doctors here say it would be prohibitively expensive undergoing tests without medical insurance. I can't go on like this indefinitely, Jana.'

'Oh, honey, I know. I just hate the thought of you being ill on your own, without me there to take care of you.'

'Mum and Dad will be able to meet me at Gatwick,' he said. 'And at least I know the staff at the Churchill.'

Phil flew home on 13th January and whilst he was being 'sorted out' in the John Warin Ward, I put all my energies into sorting out our flat in Chêne-Bourg and in making a home for him to return to. In the meantime, we communicated by telephone.

'They've put me on steroids,' Phil said.

By the second week, he was feeling greatly improved, though he warned me not to expect too much. A week later, he arrived back in Switzerland. In a wheelchair. And with crutches.

* * *

I was shocked at the extent of his physical deterioration; naked, he looked like something out of Belsen, his ribcage skeletal and his skin hanging in empty, fleshless folds.

'You haven't got a bum any more,' I teased, to cover my concern.

Within days, Phil had a bad rectal bleed and was admitted to hospital for a transfusion. It appeared that the constant purging caused by the diarrhoea had weakened the wall of a vein in the large bowel.

Then in early February, Dr Wintsch had good news.

'The lab have found a bug in the last stool sample I submitted,' she told us.

'That's good news?' I asked.

'Certainly. Now we'll be able to treat the problem effectively.'

Sure enough, Phil was given medication which completely stopped the diarrhoea. And at last, released from its debilitating effects, he slowly began to regain some strength in his legs and was able to get about the flat on his crutches.

A wheelchair was still necessary for longer excursions, however, and it was obvious that the small car I had in mind to purchase would be totally unsuitable. With Glaxo's help we negotiated a loan that enabled us to buy something with a big boot, and the following week took possession of a Ford Sierra.

A visit from Phil's younger sister, Patrina, marked the end of February and by the time she left a week later, there were definite signs that Phil was well on the road to recovery. As his strength returned and he was less reliant on the wheelchair, he was increasingly able to turn his attention to work, and to equipping his empty lab.

'Now I've mastered the crutches and can get about a bit on my own, I can at last begin fitting it out the way I want it,' he said with satisfaction.

Gradually, as a family, we acclimatised to our new place of abode, and as I became more adept in handling Phil's wheelchair, so we became more adventurous. Towards the end of the month, we managed a weekend in Zermatt, to celebrate our sixth wedding anniversary. True to form, Phil wanted to scale every mountain peak and was less interested in enjoying the view than in reaching the top.

'Have a heart!' I reminded him. 'This wheelchair isn't motorised, you know.'

Early in April, when Phil went to the hospital for a routine check-up, he learned that he was to be transferred from Dr Wintsch, who had departed for Nepal, to Dr Bernard Hirschel who was the consultant to whom Rita had spoken on Phil's behalf.

He impressed us immediately as a man of integrity, authority, concern and compassion. Although not conventionally handsome, he was a most attractive man, with dark unruly hair, and a lopsided smile which instantly put us at ease. Reserved and quietly spoken, he had an excellent command of the English language. We heard later that he was, in fact, a very public figure – a pundit much sought after by the media, who made frequent appearances on television and was oft quoted in the press.

Day by day, we discovered new aspects of our life together in Geneva and, increasingly, we continued to feel the presence of God as we attempted to seek His will. One day, a guest speaker at church made a statement that stuck in my mind: 'Hope is the memory of the future.' More and more, I found that to be true for Phil and for me; our hope and trust in God were proving, experientially, that God is Good.

One day, Simonne took me to a dinner put on by the International Christian Women's Club. It was intended for outreach – a function to which one could bring unbelievers in order that they could hear from different speakers what God had done in their lives. Afterwards, I turned to Simonne to share my own experience of His love.

'It's strange. In spite of the fact that I know I shall be a widow sooner rather than later, I find that for the most part, I have no fear of the future.'

'You're a wonderful witness,' she said. 'Not many people have to face a situation like AIDS. But you cope so well.'

'We certainly couldn't do it alone,' I said, emphatically. 'God helps us to deal with the problems as they arise – day by day. And we know that He'll continue to do so.'

Phil and I frequently discussed the possibilities as to why God had brought us to Geneva – as we believed He had – and were aware that we must be alert, and watch for opportunities to serve Him. We were aware, too, of the evidence in our own lives of Romans 8:28 which says that 'in all things God works for the good of those who love Him.' Through Phil's disease and all the accompanying heartaches and trials, He had brought about changes for the better: good out of evil.

One of the best things was the improved communication that had grown between Phil and me as I'd learned to set aside my tendency to bottle up negative feelings. In the past they had threatened to erupt in a wave of resentment; how much better it was, I discovered, to be open and honest, and to talk through my emotional response to each issue as and when it arose. Then, together, Phil and I were able to pray – either for solutions, or simply for the strength to accept the *status quo*.

This practice had removed from me the dangers of isolation, of feeling misunderstood – and thus in opposition to Phil. Sharing put us both on the same side. What had been simply *my* problem became *our* problem. And any conflict potential was effectively defused.

However, it would be wrong to suggest that we floated on the soft scents of a spiritual rosebed. I found it hard to see Phil in so much pain. In addition, there were times when it was almost impossible for me to face up to the fact that our days on earth together were numbered. Although there were ample reminders of God's blessings, I still waged a spiritual battle against self-pity for all that I had lost.

Natasha's third birthday, closely followed by Mothering Sunday and all that that entailed, were cause for gratitude and I thanked God daily for the joys and demands of my small daughter. Meeting her needs was a great help in keeping some sort of normality in our lives. Paradoxically, however, her presence was also a reproach to my continuing frustration. And with the progression of Simonne's pregnancy came a resurgence of my hankering for another baby.

*　　*　　*

'I know I'm lucky to have Natasha, but I still desperately want a second child.'

It was July and I was seated in the office of a Dr Irion with whom I had been put in touch by Dr Hirschel.

'Have you thought of artificial insemination?' he asked.

I sighed. Here we go again, I thought. Did no one understand?

'It's Phil's baby I want,' I said despairingly. 'It has to be his.'

'You already have a daughter, I believe? Did you not have any fears when you became pregnant?'

'No.' I looked the doctor square in the eye. 'I know there could have been complications. And I'm grateful that there weren't and that Natasha's a healthy little girl. But that doesn't help.'

Dr Irion scribbled a note then continued his interrogation. Finally, he sat back and gazed at me appraisingly.

'Your case is most unusual,' he said, at last. 'Normally I have to deal with women who are already pregnant and who have become infected with the HIV virus. I'm afraid there is no risk-free method of conception, Mrs Godfrey.'

A lump rose in my throat and I barely heard the remainder of his discourse. Reluctantly, I dragged myself to my feet, shook him by the hand and returned home. This, I thought, had to be one of the hardest things to come to terms with.

For days I wrestled in prayer, seeking God's will on the matter. When Simonne was delivered of a healthy baby boy, whom she and Steve named Joseph, I was racked with jealousy. Although prior to his birth I had organised a baby shower for Simonne, I now found it incredibly difficult to face her. Visiting her, in the Clinique des Grangettes, I could hardly bring myself to look into the crib; and the cursory attention I paid her was curt to the point of rudeness.

Miserably, I confessed to Phil.

'I'm so envious. And my conscience is troubling me. Please would you explain to Steve . . . '

Phil had coped wonderfully in the last month or so, I thought, taking in a church retreat at Crêt-Bérard and a scientific conference in France where he had presented several projects. However, we were both tired and were looking forward to a spot of leave. I was to fly to the US with Tash to spend some time with my family; and Phil, after a brief stopover with his parents in England, was to join us later.

'I think I'd better take your needles and medicines in case you're refused entry,' I said. This was a distinct possibility because Phil had no American citizenship, nor was there any possibility of his obtaining medical travel insurance. Although Rita Gloor had been wonderful in sorting our health cover for all but ten per cent of Phil's medication, there the insurance company had drawn the line.

In the event, the only mishap when Phil eventually joined me in America was that his flight was delayed and then his luggage went astray. A minor tragedy!

For a week in August, we went camping in Connecticut with my sister Wendy, her husband Mike and daughter Tawny. Following that, Phil and I flew to San Diego for a holiday on our own. Although we greatly enjoyed the rest and the sightseeing, by the time we returned to Switzerland on 18th August, the baby problem was as acute as ever. We were both depressed.

When Natasha started school at the jardin d'enfants, my feelings were further inflamed. Towards the middle of September, I knew I could not go on like this. Earnestly I prayed that God would intervene; that He would give me some sort of definite answer that would bring me peace.

He did. It was 'No.'

*   *   *

It was quite clear; like a spoken voice in my head. At first I tried to convince myself that this might mean 'No, not yet.' Deep down, however, I knew that God had taken me at my word and that although His answer was not what I'd hoped for, it was at least decisive and unambiguous. Once I'd worked through the ramifications in my own mind, I was able to share with Phil.

'I'm sad for Tash,' I said, thinking of Phil's mum, who had lost her only sister as a child, and of his dad and mine, both of whom were only-children. 'But it's funny. Now that I've had a final answer from God – even though it was No – I feel absolutely at peace about it.'

Phil covered my hand with his. 'I'm glad you've reached that point, Jana. You know how I've always felt. It had to be your decision whether or not to have children, because you were the one at risk.'

'But it was good, wasn't it, to have an excuse for proper sex? We'll miss that . . . '

Silently and guiltily, I found myself wondering if I would ever marry again and have a second family, should anything happen to Phil. Then I pushed the thought from my mind.

Next day, as soon as I'd taken Tash to school, I bundled up my maternity clothes and took them down to the American Women's Club Thrift Shop to be sold. There was no going back.

*   *   *

With a decision made, I found myself better able to cope with my jealousy of Simonne, and began to confide in her again.

'I really miss the help around the house that Phil used to give me before he lost the use of his legs,' I said to her one day. 'He used to do most of the hoovering, and sometimes he'd help with the cooking too.'

Simonne burped the baby over her shoulder. 'I can understand that,' she said with feeling. 'I couldn't manage without Steve's help. He does most of the washing up.'

'Oh, I can't trust Phil with that,' I said. 'He's not thorough enough for my liking – never uses enough hot water. I've tried to put it in terms of cleaning test tubes – he knows that's essential if his experiments aren't to be ruined. But I haven't made much headway.'

'Still. He's very good with Tash, isn't he?'

'Sure. But he can't do as much as he used to. When we ʼed in Oxford he'd bath her, or take her a walk while I cooked dinner. It's harder for him to keep an eye on her now because she knows she can get away with anything and he can't stop her.'

Although talking to Simonne helped me to let off steam, I felt greatly deprived of the professional advice that had been available in Oxford. The periodic visits from Mary, our social worker, had been a yardstick against which to measure my actions and reactions. Here in Geneva, it seemed to me that though everyone was very concerned about Phil's emotional and practical capabilities, mine were of no importance. I decided to have a word with Dr Philippe de Moerloose who was head of the haemophilia department in Geneva.

'I wondered if there was a support group amongst the haemophiliacs?' I asked.

'You mean those infected with HIV?'

I nodded. 'Yes. I think we'd both find it helpful to be put in touch with others in the same boat.'

The doctor pursed his lips. 'I'm afraid not. There are too few to make a group. Besides, if they're not actually ill, they don't want to think about it. However, I can put you in touch with SIDA Genève.'

SIDA was the French equivalent of AIDS and to my Anglicised ears, was more acceptable than the English version. Since our arrival in Geneva, I'd found it infinitely preferable to think of Phil in these terms – as a SIDA victim, rather than as having AIDS.

As soon as I could, I took myself into town to see the Centre's *directrice*, Brigitte Studer. She was a slender woman in her forties, with an attractive heart-shaped face, accentuated by a centre parting in her dark hair, which she wore in a shoulder-length bob.

On the way to her office she showed me through a room which overlooked the street two floors below, and which was brightly decorated with paintings and crafts. A coffee machine, notice board and settee were set against the walls, and a large white oval table, surrounded by dozen chairs, dominated the remaining space. This w

the 'drop-in centre' where anyone – sufferers, friends
or family members – could come in off the street quite
spontaneously whenever they felt in need of a chat, or a
shoulder to cry on.

Once we were seated in Brigitte's office, I told her
Phil's story. Her English was little better than my French
but somehow we managed to communicate and she was
very sympathetic of our plight. The Centre, she told me,
had been opened in 1987, in response to overwhelming
pressures. Per head of population, Switzerland had the
highest percentage in Europe of people infected with the
HIV virus, and those suffering full-blown AIDS. When I
expressed surprise, Brigitte explained that drug abuse was
a major problem, made prevalent by a highly transient
population.

'Geneva is a centre of commerce, with many international companies, all of which need a workforce,' she said,
searching for words. 'It's an attractive place for people to
come to take up employment, and therefore, a captive
market for the drug pushers. Also, our medical facilities
are excellent – another attraction.'

The Centre's objectives, she told me, were two-fold:
preventative and supportive. Staff consisted of two pro-
fessionals employed by the Canton – of whom she was one
– plus another thirty or so volunteers, most of whom either
knew of someone who was HIV positive, or someone who
was in a high risk group.

Various victim-support groups met at different times of
the week, in an informal, self-directing manner, though
nothing existed solely for the benefit of wives and families.
Brigitte suggested that in view of the problems I had
experienced in coming to terms with not having another
baby, I might find the women's group helpful.

Then shortly before I left, she told me of a conference
that was scheduled to take place the following month in
Crêt-Bérard.

'Christopher Spence of London Lighthouse is coming
ver with a team, to run a series of seminars for us,' she

said. 'Do try and come. It will be in English with French translations, because, of course, most of the participants will be French-speaking Swiss.'

Thanking her warmly for her help, I took my leave. On my way home, I enrolled for a class at Migros in Advanced French. I didn't want to miss anything at that conference!

*   *   *

The conference was on 4th October. Prior to that, Phil had some meetings at Glaxo UK and, in order to join him, I travelled by car with Phil's mum and dad when they returned to England after visiting us. It was good to spend time with Phil's sister, Paulette, to see old friends, to check on our house in Percy Street and to fit in a service at St Aldate's on the Sunday. However, by the time we returned to Geneva, Phil was again having problems with diarrhoea. The day before we were due to go to Crêt-Bérard, I took him into work after lunch, then had to collect him early that afternoon, because he'd been caught short.

The next morning he had his work assessment.

'I hope it's okay,' he said as I packed for the weekend. 'I'm feeling really nervous. I've missed so much time at work . . .'

In the event, the review board were concerned only in respect of how they might best help him to work from our flat, on those occasions when he felt physically under par and was unable to get in to the lab. He returned home greatly relieved.

Despite our policy of silence, we had eventually decided to tell Derek and Beryl of Phil's condition in order that they could pray more effectively, and had broken the news over dinner at our place. We'd left it to their discretion as to whom they should divulge the information and later, had learned from the youth pastor that they were firmly protective of our privacy. They were als very supportive in arranging practical help when we needed it.

A family from church had agreed to have Tash for the duration of the conference and that afternoon, after dropping her off with the Martis, Phil and I set off in the car.

Crêt-Bérard was between Lausanne and Montreux, about an hour and a half's drive from Geneva and had been the venue for the church retreat we had attended a couple of months previously. A stone-walled, rambling old building, it comprised a large conference hall and an accommodation block which looked over the mountains. In view of Phil's wheelchair dependence, we were allocated a bedroom in the cloisters, that opened on to a broad terrace with a circular fishpond and tiny fountain, beyond which was a small chapel. Eagerly, I drank in the peace and tranquillity.

The conference provided me with my first opportunity to meet other people who were HIV positive, amongst them drug addicts and homosexuals. Phil, it transpired, was the only haemophiliac. It seemed to me that he was also the most far advanced, in terms of the AIDS virus. I don't know what I had expected, but somehow that hit me hard. The other delegates looked so healthy by comparison.

The aim of the weekend workshop was to show people with the HIV virus how they could deal with the changes that the disease would inevitably bring about in their lives. One of the core ideas was to put yourself at the centre of your life, rather than seeking to please your family, friends, doctors and so on.

As one of the team put it: 'Instead of thinking "how will others think about me or react to me?" you can begin to consider how you can be in control of the decisions that affect you.'

We began, as instructed, by imagining ourselves as babies – the centre of our Being. From there we moved out to the conditional love of childhood – the parental actions that signal approval of our actions; and from there to our ultimate dependence on others for the perception of our selves and their evaluation of our worth.

We were encouraged to draw a diagram, with Self at the centre like the hub of a wheel and, radiating out like spokes, the people and ideas on whom we depended. Phil and I put 'Faith in God' as the largest of our spokes, with each other, our families, friends and fellowship named individually alongside.

Finally, we were shown that each of us was capable of reclaiming our Self, of taking charge of our lives, of facing the problems of AIDS moment by moment, and of taking in hand the decisions that would affect us personally.

Looking around, I couldn't help thinking how much better people would be able to cope if they put God in the centre of their lives instead of Self. There was no sense of arrogance or superiority in my analysis, but I had a strong feeling that we had something the others had not – a power from both without and within. And that in the Holy Spirit, we had been given the grace not simply to accept or resign ourselves to our situation, but to use it dynamically to change our lives for the better and to glorify God.

My feelings were borne out at the next workshop. We formed a circle, then each person was invited to step into the middle and to say how they had been oppressed.

'Oppression divides people,' the group leader said, 'so that they no longer take care of one another. I'd like all those who identify with the one in the middle, to join him or her, to symbolise your support.'

Some felt that being female was in itself a form of oppression; others cited drugs, a working-class background and, of course, the HIV virus and AIDS. It broke my heart to see Phil, frail and gaunt in his wheelchair, identifying with the last category. Then it was my turn. I stepped into the centre of the circle.

'Personally,' I said, 'I have no experience of oppression – other than as a Christian.'

As with the others, everyone clapped.

'One of the reasons I came here,' I continued, 'was to learn. But it was also to share. I want people to know why we're not afraid of the future. We know that Phil is going to heaven. And we know that God is caring for us, and that He will supply all my needs after Phil is gone.'

There was silence. Then one by one, as we disbanded, many of the delegates expressed their awareness of the strength that we possessed, and told us that it was evident in our demeanour. I felt a wonderful sense of achievement.

Later, when we returned to our room, I shared my elation with Phil.

'The workshop was a very good experience, wasn't it?'

He agreed with enthusiasm. 'But it's jolly tiring, too,' he said, collapsing on to the bed. 'I feel whacked out with having to concentrate so hard.'

'Me too.' I flopped down beside him. 'I didn't want to miss anything but it *was* pretty intense.' Most of the folks we'd met spoke nothing but French, and much of the time we'd been in support groups of only four.

Phil turned towards me. 'I enjoyed talking to the Lighthouse team. That was very helpful. They run a drop-in centre in London.'

'It was being able to express my feelings to other women about difficult, personal issues that meant most to me,' I said. To begin with I had found it particularly difficult to communicate my emotions in a foreign language and had been glad of the help of a girl called Isabelle. She had been able to translate for me.

Phil rolled on to his back and we lapsed into silence. Staring at the ceiling, I recalled how I'd felt compelled, during one of the sessions, to give a hug to one of the self-professed bisexuals. It was quite out of character for me. But when I'd shared my inner urge with the group leader, I'd been disappointed when he had asked me to wait until the end of the seminar before carrying out my intention. Nevertheless, though the feeling had been diminished by the delay, I'd been aware of the need to be obedient to what I believed was the prompting of the Holy

Spirit. Later, I'd clumsily, but sincerely, put my thought into action.

'That incident with Michel . . . ' I said, rolling over on the bed to look at Phil, 'perhaps my impulse to give him a hug was more for my benefit than his?'

Phil turned on his side and looked at me quizzically. 'How do you mean?' he asked.

'Well – perhaps it wasn't so much that he needed to feel accepted and acceptable . . . Perhaps it was me who needed my inhibitions broken down?'

*   *   *

Three days after our return home, Phil was due for a check-up with Dr Hirschel at the hospital and, to my dismay, was kept in for a transfusion. To begin with TB was suspected and Natasha had to undergo a test to see if she was a carrier. The results showed her to be clear, and Phil was then discovered to have a pulmonary disease known as microbacterium kansaii.

As soon as he was released, David, Paulette and the boys arrived for a five-day visit and when they departed, Glaxo had a computer installed in the bedroom for Phil's use, so that he could work from home.

My thirty-fifth birthday fell later in the month and to celebrate we dined at Cheval-Blanc, a formal Italian restaurant in Vandoeuvres, near Chêne-Bourg. Autumn winds had wrenched the leaves from the trees and sent them scurrying down the streets, where they congregated in sorry-looking mounds that seemed to be fearfully awaiting the next gust to dispatch them once more. Under the advance of Phil's wheelchair, they made a crushed, sibilant whisper.

Phil was not feeling well. He gave scant attention to the menu and ordered his meal with a perfunctory disregard for preference. By the time I had finished my veal, he had toyed so long with his plate of pasta, that it had congealed into a solid glutinous lump. It was a depressing sight.

'This is meant to be a happy occasion,' I said, resentfully. Was there no aspect of our lives together that was beyond the destructive power of this damnable disease?

Phil laid down his fork. His shoulders were hunched up and his head hung forward. For a moment he appeared to be struggling with himself. Then he glanced, briefly, at me.

'I find it so hard . . . ' he faltered, pressing his fingers to his eyes.

My own filled in response and I reached across the table to touch his hand. 'I know, honey. It's hard for me too.'

'It's knowing . . . ' he gulped and choked back the tears, 'It's knowing that I won't be around . . . Knowing the birthdays are limited . . . Knowing I won't see Tash growing up . . . '

All around us diners were busily engaged in the serious and the not so serious business of eating and talking. A hum filled the air. Only at our table was life temporarily suspended. Curtailed by a future that yawned – an empty abyss.

Phil would never know Tash the child – grown out of infancy into that era of discovery and excitement in the world around her. Lost to him were the years of innocence, that precious trust of a daughter in her father. He would not experience the heartaches of her adolescence, the first, tentative explorations of her emotions and her spirit. Nor would he share the joys of seeing them made captive to man and to God.

And what of Natasha, herself? Denied the balance of two parents, as God had ordained, would she grow up with a lopsided view of life? A future filtered only through the perceptions of me, her mother? Could I take God at His word? Trust Him to be truly a 'defender of widows and a father to the fatherless'?

Somehow, I knew that I could. Covertly, I dabbed at my eyes with my napkin. Then I reached again for Phil's hand. 'I'll never let her forget you, hon,' I whispered. 'I ~omise. I'll never let her forget . . . '

7

View from the Valley

Even though I walk through the valley of the shadow of death, I will fear no evil, for you are with me; your rod and your staff, they comfort me.

Psalm 23:4

In that winter of 1990–1, Geneva lay under a mantle of grey cloud that hugged the shores of Lac Léman and blotted the sun from the narrow twisting streets and cobbled squares of the Old Town. All around, however, was a different story. A trip out of the city revealed a sky of silky blue, against which, mountain peaks of dazzling white cut a jagged edge.

A similar phenomenon became apparent in our lives. Every so often, when the gloomy pall of Phil's illness lifted, sunshine was disclosed in other quarters. And with it came a greater clarity of our situation. Then, face to face with the brevity of our future together, we would find ourselves moving into an era of closer companionship, when the conventions and inhibitions of life would fall away – superfluous.

Deprived by Phil's diminished libido of sexual intercourse as an expression of our oneness, we found our spiritual harmony in other avenues. Gradually we developed a new sensitivity to one another, that drew us into fresh depths of intimacy. And we found that we were able to talk about anything and everything, unashamed to be seen in all our weaknesses.

One day, early in the New Year, I came across Phil crying. I habitually woke early and made tea for us both, while Tash slumbered on – as loth as her daddy to be dragged from sleep.

Phil was hunched against the bedhead when I re-entered the room.

'What is it, hon?' I asked, with alarm. 'Is the pain bad?'

It was a foolish question. There was never a time when Phil was not racked with pain. It was apparent in every movement of his limbs. Setting down two steaming mugs of tea, I longed to be able to communicate my understanding with some physical gesture of affection. However, one of the most frustrating aspects of this illness – perhaps more so than being denied sexual contact – was that even a simple hug or a kiss could cause Phil untold suffering.

Nevertheless, he reached out for me and, gingerly, I put my arms around him. For a few moments, we clung together whilst he struggled to control himself. Then he fell back against the pillow and rubbed a hand over his face with a weary gesture of defeat.

'I don't feel I can face work today,' he said in flat tones.

I held out a mug of tea. 'C'mon. Drink this. You'll feel better then . . . '

He shook his head and closed his eyes. Tears squeezed weakly from beneath the lids. 'I'm just . . . tired . . . ' he said. 'Tired of fighting.'

I put my hand over his. 'But you're doing so well, honey.'

I knew that Phil tried to be strong for me. At his insistence we were in the process of applying for his Swiss driving licence – an arduous task if ever there was one, involving treks to photo booths and opticians, not to men- ion mountains of Swiss bureaucracy. And only weeks ago, ortly before Christmas, he'd attended the Glaxo party.

'D'you remember?' I asked him. 'You even managed a dance – one arm over my shoulder and the other over Simonne's. I was so proud of you, Phil.'

Again, he shook his head. 'My whole body feels like it's had enough.'

He lay, slumped on the mattress, and it was easy to see that he meant what he said.

'Sometimes I feel so sleepy . . . ' he went on. 'I get the feeling that I could drop off . . . and never wake up.'

I found such talk scary. 'Are you . . . are you afraid?' I asked.

'Of death?' He opened his eyes and considered. 'Not so much of dying,' he said, at last. 'Only of leaving you and Tash.'

Struggling hard to contain my tears, I went to the window, threw back the shutters, and stared out at the brook that flowed from the leat beneath the road. There was barely a trickle. And I thought of the mountain snows that fed it, now hard-packed and icy. In spring, when the thaw came, it would be in full spate, gushing down the valley . . .

'When I'm gone,' Phil went on, 'you should get married again. If you find someone you love.'

'Oh, honey . . . ' I could contain myself no longer. I turned and, kneeling at the side of the bed, I put my head on his hands and wept. What would the end be like for Phil, I wondered? Would he be called upon to suffer unimaginable agonies? And if so, would I cope with the demands made upon me? Physically? Emotionally?

And afterwards? When his tormented body was at rest, could I go on? Would we each, in our own way, be able to endure to the last?

Down below, outside the *pâtisserie* a flock of sparrows began a noisy altercation – no doubt over some scraps of stale croissant thrown out daily by the *pâtissier*.

Jesus had drawn a comparison between His disciples and sparrows. 'Do not be afraid of those who kill the body but cannot kill the soul,' He'd said. 'Are not two sparrows so for a penny? Yet not one of them will fall to the ground apart from the will of your Father.'

Then He'd finished by saying: 'Don't be afraid; you are worth more than many sparrows.'

When Phil and I had cried ourselves out, we drew apart and I wiped my eyes. 'We must take one day at a time,' I said firmly, and reached for the tea.

Phil took his mug, gulped at the contents then set it down on the floor. He cleared his throat. 'Still, I'd like to make some plans . . . ' he said. 'A memorial service . . . Back home – in Oxford?'

I looked at him, searchingly. What he said made sense. How much better it would be for him to have a say in his farewell to those who loved him, than for me to have to guess at his wishes. And planning this service would bring home, as nothing else could, the ongoing nature of Phil's life in eternity. His arrangements would be as for a journey: a passing from one place to another; a celebration of his life on earth and of his elevation to a higher plane of being – in the presence of God, Himself.

Quickly, I found myself caught up with his ideas and for the next half-hour we talked – falteringly to begin with, but gaining in strength with each moment – of hymns and choruses, Bible readings and friends.

And later, in keeping with my need to bring order out of chaos, I listed Phil's choices and preferences in my personal organiser file. I marked the section 'Phil.'

*   *   *

It would have been easy to give in to Phil's desire to cocoon himself in bed whenever he was in a negative frame of mind, but I was aware that this was not always the best policy to adopt, and that 'kindness' of this nature might not be the most beneficial for him. Sometimes, I felt I had to take a very different stance.

'I'll drive you over to the lab, honey,' I would say, with

all the firmness of a mother taking a malingering child to school.

Afterwards, he would express his gratitude and tell me, when I collected him at the end of the day, that the sense of achievement had been worth the effort.

It was difficult to know, however, which of us found these occasions the more draining and, inevitably, there were times when my patience wore thin. Then I'd find myself saying brusquely: 'It's no good wallowing in self-pity. You should pull yourself out of it. Or at least concentrate on something else.'

When Phil did complain, which was not often, it was only ever about pain and never about the things denied him. 'I try not to think about that too much,' he'd say. 'It only makes me depressed.'

My conscience would prick and I'd attempt to make amends. 'I don't mean to be unfair, honey. It's just that when you're down it wears me down. And then I'm no help to you.'

I was tired. For the entire fourteen months since his pneumocystis, Phil had rarely slept through the night without coughing. That meant that I, too, often had interrupted sleep. When Tash also developed a cough that kept us awake, I found it increasingly difficult to cope. After some weeks, I decided that there was only one solution.

'I'm going to have to move into the spare room,' I said.

Phil's response echoed my own. 'This disease is ruining our marriage,' he said resentfully.

'Boss!' My voice crept up a note. 'I don't like it either, but I can't go on like this night after night.'

On a good day, we would get to bed at about eleven o'clock. From then until dawn, Phil would be up once or twice, for an hour at a time, with diarrhoea, and a further five or six times with cramps in his legs. In the morning, I would take him a cup of tea, get Natasha ready for school, and catch up on shopping and household chores whilst he slept on.

At about ten-thirty I'd give him breakfast in bed, after which he would again have to grapple for an hour or so on the toilet. When I'd collected Natasha from school, I would then help him to dress – most often in a pair of soft, baggy jogging pants which put no pressure on his abdomen or limbs – then carry him into the living-room. I'd fix a light lunch, then at about two-thirty, I'd take Phil into work, carrying him down the winding flight of stone steps from our flat to the car, then returning for his wheelchair. At five-thirty or six, it would be time to fetch him home again and, whilst he dozed in front of the TV, I would put Natasha to bed and prepare supper, which we would eat around eight or nine o'clock in the evening. Frequently, by the time I keeled over into bed once more, I would wonder, secretly, if life would ever again have any purpose beyond that of coping with sickness and pain.

Such thoughts stemmed mainly from fatigue. But if there were serious doubts about purpose, they were soon to be addressed. A week later, we heard, via a telephone call from Phil's parents, that a publisher was interested in our story. They wanted us to write a book!

'They suggest that you try to get something down on tape,' Dad said down the line. 'Put something together showing the positive aspects of your experience.'

'That's all very well,' Phil said to me when we rang off. 'But it's very hard when you're the one going through it. It's difficult to see anything positive coming out of suffering.'

His tone was reflective rather than self-pitying and it was obvious that the idea had captured his imagination.

'There must be something you've learned that you can pass on to others going through the same thing,' I said, encouragingly. 'After all, look at the number of people who comment on your courage.'

Phil snorted. 'Frankly,' he said, 'I don't see how that could be of encouragement to anyone since it doesn't help me one iota! No. The whole issue of AIDS triggers questions about the wider aspects of suffering in general.

But in the end, the only one that matters for someone in my position is: "Why me, particularly? Why should I be given this horrible disease?"'

For a moment, Phil paused. Then he said, 'I'm not sure that I can answer that. All I can say with any certainty, is that God knows. And He loves me. And one day I shall be with Him. And then, perhaps, I shall know too.'

The simplicity of his rhetoric spoke volumes, and suddenly, his pain and our mutual suffering seemed to have a fresh focus. With the realisation that there was a whole generation of AIDS victims and their families who had heard nothing of Jesus or of eternal life, came a new objective. We knew, that as Christians, we had something worth sharing.

* * *

Throughout February, Phil underwent exhaustive tests with a gastroenterologist in a bid to discover the cause of his bowel disorder. And as the month drew to a close, Dr Hirschel recommended a period of convalescence at the Clinique Genevoise in Montana.

The Clinique was a huge building, set into the side of a mountain and surrounded by snow-laden pine forests. Phil had a private room on the third floor, with access to the terrace at the front. In order that I might accompany him, Mum and Dad had made a flying visit to Geneva and taken Natasha back home with them so once I had seen Phil comfortably settled, I installed myself in the nearby Villa Notre Dame.

As well as treatment for the diarrhoea, attempts were made to build Phil's appetite. Fresh air and exercise were an important part of the programme and each day turned into an adventure of sightseeing. However, it was debatable as to whose appetite was most boosted, and which of us was the more vigorously exercised, as I heaved and pushed the wheelchair, bearing Phil's gaunt and emaciated body, up hill and down dale!

For a special, early birthday treat, I arranged for Phil to have a trip in a hot-air balloon – and had a hard job winning over a very nervous operator when he saw the frailty of his would-be passenger. At last he relented. And by the time Phil returned, tired but exhilarated, he had earned the admiration of both the balloonist and his assistant, not to mention that of the skiers on the *piste* where he landed.

One day we took a gondola to Les Violettes. For someone in Phil's condition there was a fair distance to walk from the *télécabine* to the *téléphérique* which would take us on to la Plaine Morte, but he was insistent. Gamely, he struggled on his crutches, dodging skiers as best he could, and panting for breath in the thin atmosphere.

'C'mon, Phil. Nearly there,' I said, encouragingly. And suddenly, I was reminded of Dad's words, the day we'd told him of Phil's infection.

'Phil always insists upon scaling the heights,' he'd said, 'mentally, emotionally and physically.'

I'd experienced that grit and determination in Phil when we'd been fell climbing in the Lake District, where he had always urged me onward and upward: 'Come on, Jana. Nearly there . . . ' Exactly as I'd just said to him.

Then I would complain good-naturedly, 'We don't have to belt all the way to the top in one go, you know. It's good to be able to stop sometimes, to enjoy the view.'

There were parallels to be drawn, I thought, and realised with a rush of pleasure, how changed our priorities had become compared to the early years of our marriage. No longer was I so intent upon wanting to be proved right, and to have my efforts recognised; nor was I nearly as sulky as I once had been.

'It's amazing the good things that can come out of such a bad situation, isn't it?' I said, when we finally reached the cable-car station.

Phil propped himself against a wooden post and nodded, his brow furrowed. 'What sort of things do you see as good?'

'Well . . . The opportunity to write this book for one. And . . . just feeling closer to you.' I paused, then added: 'And having people get to know you better because you're more willing to share.'

Everyone had been so helpful and supportive, I reflected. Our friends, the Arkinstalls, thought nothing of arriving at our flat with a rented video for Phil whilst they took Tash and me for an afternoon's skiing with them at Les Caroz d'Arâches, in France. Nor, on other occasions, did they hesitate to have Natasha over to play with Emilie, in order that Phil and I could have time together alone.

The staff and personnel at Glaxo couldn't have been kinder, either. I had only to mention a difficulty with Swiss officialdom, and they would take it upon themselves to help. Only the previous week, when I'd approached the insurance company regarding an unpaid bill for Factor VIII, and had been unable to comprehend the explanation I'd been given, Véronique had taken the matter up on my behalf.

'We've a lot to be thankful for,' I said, as we gazed across the snow-clad peaks.

'Yep!' Phil nodded in agreement. 'God has been good to us.'

We stood in silence for a moment, then he let go of one crutch and caught hold of my hand. His voice, when he spoke, was gruff.

'I honestly don't think I could have survived this long, without you,' he said. 'You stop me dwelling on the pain – and the problems. And you pull me out when I'm feeling down . . . '

I shrugged. 'I only do what anyone would do for someone they love . . . '

Sunlight picked out the spangled colours of distant skiers on the *piste* and overhead, the cables dipped and hummed at the approach of the *téléphérique*.

'I – I never knew what you saw in me,' Phil said, shyly. 'I never thought – as a haemophiliac – that I could ever be attractive to a woman . . . '

Laughing through my tears, I swung his hand in mine, leaned carefully towards him and gently kissed his mouth. 'I never knew what you saw in me, either,' I said.

Then Phil took up his crutches and, together, we headed on up the mountain.

*   *   *

Within a fortnight of being discharged from the Clinique, and with no improvement of his bowel problem, Phil was again admitted to hospital – this time for a bacterial pneumonia.

'I have to be out by Friday 1st March,' he told Dr Hirschel. 'We're flying back to the UK for my mother's sixtieth birthday. It's a surprise party.'

And what a surprise it was for her to find Phil there, with a short speech prepared, and a toast proposed from his wheelchair! Dr Hirschel and the ward doctor had taken some convincing that Phil was up to the trip but his determination had won the day.

Walking – even with the aid of crutches – was now virtually impossible for Phil and the wheelchair had become a necessity.

'It takes all my concentration to put one foot in front of the other,' he told me. When I heard him chatting to the attendant at Gatwick, shortly before being carried on to the plane that would take us back to Geneva, I reflected with pride, that for all the pain and indignity he endured, he complained so very little. And then only in my hearing.

'Sometimes I can cling to Jesus,' he confessed, when even the strongest pills failed to dull the pain in his guts, 'And sometimes – I can't . . . '

The stories of Job and of Daniel had impressed Phil greatly. Each had endured extraordinary hardship, yet neither had yielded to bitterness. And God, in His faithfulness, had never failed them.

A friend of Phil's parents had suggested we read Psalm

118 in which the Psalmist speaks of being 'pushed back' and 'about to fall'. Yet he knew the Lord's presence with him, knew Him as his helper, his refuge, his strength and his song. We drew comfort from the repeated refrain: 'His love endures for ever', taking that to mean that though Phil might not always be able to cling to Jesus, Jesus would never let go of him.

'"In my anguish I cried to the Lord,"' I read aloud to Phil, '"And he answered by setting me free."'

Freedom from anxiety had to be on a practical level, as far as I was concerned. I had a sense of having lost my grip on certain areas of our life. A sense, almost, of powerlessness. In an attempt to redress the balance, I felt the need to exert control where I could. Day by day, I learned to adopt various strategies to help me cope with the demands made upon me physically and found, inadvertently, a corresponding psychological spin-off.

I hated the smell of diarrhoea that pervaded every room of the flat and was a constant reminder of Phil's sickness. My solution was a liberal use of air-fresheners. I hated, too, the necessity of having the toilet roll in the living-room – in full view – and hastily tucked it out of sight whenever anyone called. I bought navy washcloths for Phil's bum – for those occasions when he didn't make it to the toilet in time – in the hope that the stains, which steadfastly refused to wash out, would at least be less noticeable.

Being 'caught short' was a recurring problem which could easily turn into a major difficulty when bedding was soiled. Although we received an allowance for extra sheets, they still had to be laundered, and use of the washing machine in the basement of the building was allotted strictly by rota: washday, for our flat, was scheduled for Friday mornings only!

In an attempt to minimise accidents – particularly at night – Tasha's training potty was put back into service, so that Phil could slide off the bed, then haul himself up by his arms when he had finished. And finally, I bought a small portable mirror so that he could sit at the sink and shave, rather than having to rely on me to hold him up. They were simple remedies; but somehow it seemed to take us a long time to rethink even the most basic of functions; and the learning was an ongoing process.

The appearance of my home had always mattered to me, with tidiness almost more important than cleanliness. Though I missed the help that Phil had given me in the past, I found, in my self-imposed regimen, a sort of grim satisfaction. Far from being tiresome, the daily grind became my salvation. Being busy kept me from morbid introspection; and the feeling, at the end of each day, that I'd accomplished something tangible, kept me cheerful against all odds.

Visiting friends, needlework – even doing the household accounts or writing a letter – seemed infinitely more beneficial to my body and mind than endless entreaties of the Lord to give me strength to endure; though perhaps, in hindsight, this was the practical outworking of His answer to such prayers.

Frequently, now, I was able to see God's wisdom in not allowing me another baby. How would I have coped, I wondered? And in the light of the full horror of Phil's illness, I thanked God from the bottom of my heart for keeping me free of infection.

* * *

'Made it! I can hardly believe it!'

It was 13th March, 1991 – Phil's thirty-fourth birthday. Like him I could hardly believe that he'd got this far. Already he had exceeded Dr Hopkin's 1987 prediction of 'three years life expectancy' by a good nine months. These days we notched up birthdays and anniversaries as major attainments.

The doorbell rang and when I went to answer it, there stood Rita Gloor.

'I have come to bring these,' she said, proffering a

beautiful bouquet of yellow roses for Phil, and a box of Swiss chocolates for Natasha and me.

I loved the way she rolled her r's and enunciated her English with just a hint of Swiss correctness. Smiling broadly, I showed her to the bedroom where Phil was, then went to the kitchen to make coffee.

'Rita, how kind,' I heard Phil say. 'You really shouldn't have bothered.'

'Just a little gift for your birthday,' she replied. 'You won't want to come in to work today . . . But tell me, how are you feeling? Really.'

Phil had done quite well recently, I thought, as I spooned coffee into the mugs I'd set on a tray. One evening he'd accompanied Tash and me to a souper soirée sponsored by our church. It had been a very international affair – like the congregation in our church – with folk from the Philippines, Jamaica, America and Britain and had been designed as a sort of outreach and social event, with hostesses providing the stock for soup, and guests supplying the vegetables. We didn't get out much as a family any more, and I'd been pleased that Phil had made the effort to go, though he'd eaten so little . . .

'It's frustrating not being able to eat,' Phil was saying to Rita as I appeared at the bedroom door. 'Jana cooks me lovely meals, and I just look at the food and can't face eating it. I feel I'm letting her down.'

I handed coffee to Rita and to Phil, then pulled up a chair on the other side of the bed. 'You said you found it a comfort to hear, from Linda, that other haemophiliacs in your condition have exactly the same problem,' I reminded him. Linda had also said, when we'd taken a trip over to the Centre after Mum's birthday party, that Phil was the longest living of any of the AIDS victims on their list.

'And what about . . . ' Rita moved one hand around in the air, delicately indicating her abdomen.

Phil sighed. 'I wish they could find out what's causing this diarrhoea,' he admitted. 'I spend three-quarters of my time in the toilet. It's very frustrating. I keep trying to think of ways I could contribute more at work but I need to be there to supervise my technician.'

'Don't worry about that,' Rita replied. 'Your contribution is very much appreciated.'

'There's always a battle with how much medication I should take,' Phil went on. 'I have a choice: no diarrhoea and bombed out of my mind; or pain and diarrhoea, but mentally more with it. Some choice. Some contribution.'

'Don't worry,' Rita said, again. 'The directors are very aware of your input: the papers you have produced, and the way your colleagues seek and value your advice. They have no qualms. In fact they are delighted.'

This was gratifying news to hear, and I flushed with pleasure on Phil's behalf.

'However,' Rita went on, 'although Jonathan says that he finds your morale astounding, he is concerned that you might be pushing yourself too hard.'

For some time she and Phil discussed work, then she left. Her visit had visibly boosted Phil's spirits and later, he was able to eat a little of the birthday cake Tash and I had made him. Then after lunch, at his request, I took him, and what remained of the cake, into work, where we found that his colleagues had laid on a little party for him, with champagne and wine. Finally, in the evening we went out for dinner – though Phil, by this time, was not feeling well.

'A bit too much birthday,' he grinned, wryly, when I put him to bed. 'But I'm glad I've made it this far.'

'So am I!' I replied.

'Are you?' he asked, catching hold of my hand and pulling me down on to the bed beside him. 'Really? Do you honestly think it's all been worth while?'

'Yes!' I said, decisively.

In the lamplight his thin, wasted body hardly made a ripple under the bedclothes and there was a frailty about his features.

'I – I need to hear that,' he said. 'Sometimes – I wonder.'

'Well don't,' I replied. 'I know I get tired sometimes. And I know I get fed up with all the extra physical work, too. But I've been blessed with a strong constitution. And when I stop and think about it – it's worth it!'

I got up, crossed the room to put out the light, and returned to bed.

'Even without thinking about it,' I said, climbing under the duvet, 'I see every extra day that we have together as a gift.'

And so it was, I thought, lying back on the pillow. A gift. A gift from God.

* * *

By the end of the week, Phil felt well enough to go to the service on Sunday. We had applied for membership some weeks previously and, as was the custom, we were to give our testimonies to the congregation. When the time came, I wheeled Phil to the front then seated myself at his side. The church was full and all eyes turned on us, expectantly.

'You go first,' I whispered.

Phil gave me an 'I knew you'd do this to me' look then faced the congregation and proceeded.

'I was brought up in a Christian family,' he began, 'so the precepts of faith were well known to me. However, my parents made it clear that I had to decide for myself: it was a decision they couldn't make for me.

'There was no instant conversion experience,' he continued. 'Just a gradual thing, as I grew up. Situations arose, in which I had to determine whether I felt that Christianity was something that was real for me. When I reached the age of twelve, I made the final decision: I felt that the evidence of Christianity was good enough to put my faith in. Although it didn't have all the answers, by any means, this idea of having someone dying for you and taking away your sin was one that I felt was very relevant to me. It could help me explain my life.'

I glanced at Phil and wondered if people would understand all that was implied in that statement. I knew that as a child he had asked God what he had done to deserve all the pain and suffering of haemophilia. And that he had eventually concluded that there was no simple explanation.

I turned my attention back to the present.

'As I've got older, my thinking has progressed,' Phil was saying. 'I've felt very strongly that without this core of Christianity, my life would be completely and absolutely meaningless. Nothing! You'd just be existing. That's what my belief in Jesus Christ, as my Saviour, gives me: meaning. Life is not just a random, scientific chance. We're not here just by some spook choice of evolution. We're actually here for a real purpose. And this certainty has grown stronger and stronger, as I've got older. It's helped my faith and given me the strength to carry on through all this illness.'

I watched, proudly, as Phil finished. Few people had been told the true nature of his disease, though I guessed it must be obvious to some. Yet there was no hint of distaste, despite Phil's emaciated condition and, as I looked out over the congregation, I saw only love and compassion written on the faces of all those good people. Many were moved to tears and, by the time I stood to give my testimony, hankies were much in evidence.

Briefly, I told everyone that I thanked God for bringing us to this church. Then I thanked them for their prayers and for the way in which they had reached out to support us with their love, throughout the time we had been in Geneva.

'All through Phil's illness,' I went on, 'I've had to learn to pray that I can listen to God. Find out what He wants me to do. Seek His will and be obedient.

And that,' I said, as I drew to a close, 'is not always easy. However, it's not we who are strong – but God in us.'

A soft, diffused glow, from the arched skylights in the ceiling high above, filled the building. It was like the aura of God.

I pushed Phil's chair back up the aisle and we resumed our places. We were part of Christ's Body universally, reflected, and particularly here in the Evangelical Baptist Church of Geneva. Not because of any ritual or ceremony, but simply because, by professing our faith in Jesus, who had died for us, He had promised that we would be 'hid' in Him, and that the Holy Spirit of God would dwell in us.

Later, when the service was over and we'd threaded our way out through the door of the church, that abstract truth was exhibited plainly in the body of believers. Derek, our pastor, and Beryl, his wife – and everyone who could press close enough in the throng that filled the sunlit courtyard – ensured that we knew a very warm welcome indeed.

*   *   *

Spring was a reminder of earlier, more active days. And as delicate Alpine flowers thrust their way out of the ground, Phil mourned the loss of his mobility and independence.

'I feel I'm letting you down,' he said, watching as I prepared lunch.

'Why's that?' I asked.

'Because I can't even walk to the park across the street with Tash any more,' he replied. 'It means I can never give you a break.'

I knew that his remark encompassed other feelings, too: sadness for the attention he would never now be able to give his daughter; the games that they would never play; the fun that was denied them. Moreover, there was a demise of dignity, of status, of parental authority. Natasha was all too aware of the fact that, as far as Daddy was concerned, she could get away with murder. Phil was quite unable to stop her.

Even so, it was not naughtiness that caused the biggest problem, but simply a lack of understanding on her part. She was constantly standing on Phil's feet, in that way that some children have, when they come up close to talk to you. Or, she would run over them with her toys – blissfully unaware of the intense pain that her daddy suffered because of her actions.

Then Phil would yell at her and she would look at him with absolute mortification written all over her impish little face, obviously mystified as to why these strange bellowing noises should be emitting from a grown man – her daddy, of all people. It all added to Phil's feelings of impotence.

I was particularly glad, therefore – for his sake as much as mine – on those occasions when he did urge me to go out, assuring me that he would cope. And it was with this in mind, that I approached Brigitte, the *directrice* of SIDA Genève. The upshot of my visit was, that in due course, she had two *benevoles* assigned to us.

Benevoles, I learned, were volunteers, people who – for compassionate reasons of their own – wanted to provide practical help for the victims and families of those suffering with AIDS. Ours were a young woman called Ruth Jones, and a young man named Francesco Trifiletti.

Ruth was British and had initially come to the Geneva area as an au pair one summer, when she had been taking an art degree. She had returned, later, to work for a Swiss company and then – perhaps as a result of a close friend who was HIV positive – had become a volunteer. Much of her work was with prostitutes – a legal profession in Switzerland. She had shoulder-length, dark curly hair and warm, dark eyes.

Francesco was in his late twenties, an Italian with black hair, an angular face and typical slim build. He was quiet and serious but came across as very caring and told us that he had lost a friend through AIDS. As with all *benevoles*, he and Ruth worked as a pair and in no time they had become firm friends. We had only to ring and they would be there – taking Tash on outings, keeping Phil company so that I could go out, or simply being a listening ear.

It was further evidence of God's love.

* * *

'Your husband is a good example of the British stiff upper lip!' Dr Hirschel told me when he saw us to arrange a blood transfusion for Phil, at the end of the month.

'He certainly doesn't complain much,' I agreed. 'I'm sure I would.'

The transfusion was a bid to give Phil a 'new lease of life' and was nicely timed to pre-date our trip to Gstaad to celebrate our seventh wedding anniversary – a further milestone along the way.

Phil's mum had said, when I'd spoken to her on the phone: 'In our family, we don't die easily,' and I'd reflected that even little James Maxted had fought on, against all odds, for nearly two years. The normal life expectancy for a baby in his condition was three months.

'Your husband's haemoglobin levels are very low,' Dr Hirschel continued, 'from fourteen down to seven. One of the reasons for his anaemia is because he's malnourished, which means that he's not making enough red blood cells. To combat that, we're going to put him on a strict high-calorie liquid diet which he will have to continue with at home. It should make life easier for him.'

And for me, I thought. Aloud, I said: 'He'll like that because he won't have to eat.'

After the transfusion, Phil looked a whole lot better.

'Hopefully, I'll put on a bit of weight with this new diet,' he said. 'And I've been given a megadose of vitamins and minerals! Intravenously, of course.'

Swallowing pills was a nightmare for Phil. He had a basketful in the drawer of his bedside table and frequently, the only way he could get them down was if I mashed some of the larger ones with a pestle and mortar, and mixed them with water.

Since the onset of his illnesses, he'd had to take antibiotics, antibacterial drugs, antifungal drugs, antitubercular drugs, antiviral drugs, antidiarrhoea drugs and steroids – not to mention the pain-killers. At one time, he was taking no less than twenty-eight per day! Not only had he difficulty in getting them down, but the schedule, too, was tiring. Some had to be taken thirty minutes before breakfast, others either three or four times daily. Remembering was a big headache and Phil sometimes complained that his entire life seemed to be governed by pills.

* * *

However, for a few days after his release, whilst we enjoyed our anniversary break in Gstaad, sickness and pills ceased to be the dominant factor in our thinking. Or at least, that was the theory. In actual fact, I had to go off sightseeing on my own because Phil was suffering severe abdominal pain and was not well enough.

His regular hospital appointment fell soon after our return home, and when Dr Hirschel saw how distended his belly was, and the pain that he was in, he booked him into Emergency.

'We're going to have to operate immediately,' Dr Hirschel said.

At that moment, Natasha decided on a game of hide and seek and vanished through the door. With no alternative but to go after her, I had to leave Phil as he was about to be moved off on a trolley into the *Urgences* (Emergency

Department). I was so cross. Tash had completely disappeared. The Hopitâl Cantonal was huge. And I wasn't at all sure how I was going to find her.

'She went that way,' said a man in the corridor. I raced through the swing doors. There was no sign of her. I searched the lifts, the wards and the stairs. After what seemed an age, I spied a large woman bearing down on me. Natasha was held firmly in her grip.

'I found her downstairs,' said the woman.

Thanking her, I grabbed at Tash's hand. 'I wanted to say goodbye to Daddy before his operation,' I said, reproachfully and rushed back to the ward.

Phil had gone. Natasha was now fretful and hungry and began playing up even more. Desperately, I wished that there were three of me – one for Phil, one for Tash and – one for me!

When I returned to the hospital that evening, I saw Phil for all of five minutes before he was wheeled away for a CT scan.

'We're going to do a colostomy,' the surgeon explained. 'That will relieve the pressure in the lower abdomen.' He paused, then went on: 'There is some sort of obstruction and we're hoping that with the scan we might be able to tell what it is.'

'Do you have any ideas?' I asked, and almost wished I hadn't.

'It could be a tumour,' the doctor said.

'Oh my goodness!' My concern must have shown.

'Lymphatic tumours are common in AIDS patients,' he explained, kindly. 'It's a relatively easy operation to perform and only takes about an hour. But of course, given your husband's recent pulmonary infection and his current state of health – it is risky.'

I took a deep breath. I had learned to live with Phil's illness and felt no stabs of fear. Earlier that month we had been studying Amos chapters four and five and I particularly liked 5:18: 'Woe to you who long for the day of the Lord.' I had sometimes wished to hasten the 'day of the Lord' for Phil, believing that if Jesus came for him, he would no longer have to suffer. Now I understood that the Lord would come when the time was right. My concern was to be only for the quality of life left to Phil.

'Is the operation really necessary?' I asked Dr Hirschel. 'I mean . . . if Phil felt like he was ready to give up . . . ?'

'This type of surgery is purely palliative,' the doctor replied. 'If we do nothing, your husband would be in considerable pain. We just want to make him more comfortable.'

So there was no question of them operating simply to prolong Phil's life? My feelings were ambivalent.

'I know Phil is trying very hard to go on living because he doesn't want to leave Tash and me,' I said.

I knew, too, that Phil was aware of how much I enjoyed being resident in Geneva and how sad I felt about the prospect of having to leave. The country was so pretty and clean. And there was so much that I still wanted to explore. Finally, I was getting to use my French after having studied it at university and during the last year had become quite fluent. In addition, there was the increase in Phil's salary which had eased our financial pressures, despite the higher cost of living in Switzerland. And I loved our pretty flat, furnished with pieces we had been able to buy with our moving allowance.

'We're talking about months now, you know,' Dr Hirschel said gently, as if reading the tumult of my mind.

I lowered my eyelids and with some diffidence, said: 'The three years that Phil was given after his pneumocystis was treated were up last June. Nine months ago! Ever since then – I've looked on each extra day as a gift.'

He nodded, understandingly, and waited while I moved off down the corridor.

Before I left that evening, Phil and I had a short prayer and a kiss. I turned at the door and looked back at him propped against the pillows. His face was white as the sheets.

'Keep fighting,' I said.

Then I swivelled on my heel and strode briskly from the ward. When I looked back again, Phil's eyes were closed.

8

A Time to Hold On

*'Strengthen the feeble hands, steady the knees
that give way; say to those with fearful hearts,
Be strong, do not fear; your God will come . . .
He will come to save you.'*

Isaiah 35:3–4

'The further into this disease we go, the more I'm convinced that God is with us,' I said to Simonne when I
returned from the hospital to collect Natasha.

She passed me a mug of tea and we sat at the table,
whilst the two little girls played on the living-room floor.

'I remember a Bible study that I did with my group in
Richmond,' I continued, 'it was on Job. It's helped me
come to terms with Phil's illness.'

Simonne eyed me thoughtfully, scooping up a recal-
citrant strand of her bobbed hair and tucking it behind
one ear. 'Yes, I can see that it would,' she said. 'Job
suffered every sort of adversity you could imagine, didn't
he . . . '

Gratified with her grasp of my comparison, I cradled my
mug in my hands and went on, eagerly: 'But the point is,
Simonne, that God was in control all along. It was only a
test of Job's faith . . . '

'Hang on, Jana,' she interrupted. 'That makes it sound
as if God puts us to the test. And I'm sure it says
somewhere in the Bible that He doesn't.'

'I didn't mean that,' I said, quickly. I wasn't sure enough of my ground to state chapter and verse, but I thought that the scripture to which she referred came somewhere at the beginning of James. 'I know that God doesn't actually *do* the tempting,' I continued. 'But He does sometimes *allow* us to be put to the test, doesn't He? I mean, according to the Bible study we did, He gave Satan permission to have a go at Job, to see how strong his faith really was.'

'Of course!' Simonne said, in her quick bright manner. 'What you're saying is that it's all part of developing patience and perseverance?'

'Right!' I nodded, put my mug down on the table and leaned forward. 'And like Job, we don't always know *why* things happen. But we do have a choice in the way we react to them.'

Silence fell between us as we considered the implications. Emilie and Tasha had disappeared, leaving a trail of dolls, books and dressing-up clothes in their wake. Gales of laughter emitting from the bedroom area of the flat indicated their whereabouts and, for a moment, we listened to be sure that all was well.

Then I said: 'Anyway, I've not spent a lot of time asking "why me?" – though I often wish Phil and I could have a normal life. Instead, I've tried to say, "I will know someday why we've gone through this." In the meantime, I'm determined not to let this disease make me angry at God.'

Deep in thought, we gazed out of the window. Across the Rhône valley the Jura mountains were a durable and magnificent reminder of God's greatness and glory.

Later, during the car journey home, I told Natasha about Phil.

'Daddy's having an operation . . . so he'll be able to eat better.' I nosed the car forward, waiting for a break in the traffic that raced into Geneva from the French border at St Julien. 'And so that he won't get such bad tummy aches,' I added.

'I got a bad pommy ache, too,' said Tash, from the back of the car.

I risked a quick glance over my shoulder and smiled as she began to recount all the illnesses she could recall having endured during her own short life! She was too young, I thought thankfully, to comprehend all the ramifications of Phil's illness.

'Hows about we say a prayer for Daddy when we get home?' I asked.

And when I tucked her into bed that night, I found that in a funny sort of way, there was a comfort in sharing. Even with a small child.

*   *   *

Phil's latest illness forced him to rethink some of the issues on which he'd already made decisions. Knowing that there was no possibility of the AIDS virus being transmitted in saliva, he had always, in the past, taken the common cup at communion. Now, however, he had second thoughts.

'I don't think I dare risk it,' he said. 'It's silly leaving myself wide open to infection. I'm quite likely to pick up everything that's going.'

Prior to Phil and I coming to Geneva – though unknown to us at the time – the church elders had met to discuss this very point. Their debate had been hypothetical in that, to their knowledge, there had been no one in the church infected with the disease, and their conclusions had been fairly predictable. There were those who were concerned for unity – which is the essence of communion – and who were, therefore, utterly opposed to the wine being served in individual cups. Others felt that the health risks represented by the common cup outweighed what was, after all, only symbolism. Eventually, after much heart-searching, a compromise was reached and a decision was made to operate both systems simultaneously. In this way, members of the church would be at liberty to choose for themselves.

Very much later, when I shared Phil's decision with Derek, he expressed surprise.

'It just goes to show how self-centred we all are, even as Christians,' he said. 'It never occurred to me or the elders to consider the risks of infection from the point of view of the AIDS victim. We thought only of the protection of those of us who are AIDS-free.'

About a week after his operation, whilst he was still in hospital, Phil intimated that he would like the elders to pray for him and Derek suggested a healing service at Phil's bedside. To my surprise, I found myself uncertain.

'It isn't that I don't have faith in healing,' I said to Derek. 'I know God is able . . . It's just . . . I'm not sure that I can believe He's going to cure Phil.'

I longed for Phil to be well, to share with me the sights and sounds of Geneva – all the things that I loved: the pretty floral displays that abounded on every square in the city centre and its environs; the sparkling, rainbowed mist of the famous *jet d'eau*; the hustle and bustle of tea rooms and cafés that spilled out on to pavements in a mêlée of white tables and chairs, dogs, waiters, weary shoppers and excited tourists; the cowbells in the mountains and the restaurants that edged Lac Léman, where the aroma of freshly cooked *filets de perches* could almost be tasted on the clean Alpine air.

'I can understand your reticence,' Derek replied, kindly. 'You believe in the possibility. But not in the probability?'

'That's it,' I said, relieved that he had grasped my meaning so clearly.

'Well, that's all right. By praying for Phil's healing, we're simply being obedient to God's command in James 5:14 "Is any one of you sick? He should call the elders of the church to pray over him and anoint him with oil in the name of the Lord."'

I knew that, because of various business commitments, organising a date that was suitable to all the elders had required some effort. In the light of their willingness to make themselves available, my ambivalence seemed all the more churlish. Diffidently, I agreed.

On this occasion, Phil had a room to himself and, despite my reservations, when the informal service went ahead on the evening of 5th April, both he and I found it a profoundly moving experience. Earnestly, I thanked God for what He had given us: our improved level of communication; the love that we had for one another; and the blessing of a beautiful daughter. Then I prayed that Jesus might always come first in our marriage.

At Phil's request, Steve Arkinstall had accompanied the church elders. Having experienced healing from cancer when he was a child he, too, was greatly moved. Each man had picked out a Scripture and prepared a few words on the text. Jack Minor had chosen Psalm 139 – that wonderful reminder that God has 'knit us together' in our mother's womb, that we are 'fearfully and wonderfully made', and that He has 'ordained all the days of our life'. There was never a time, I marvelled, when we are out of God's sight, no matter where we may go.

'If I go up to the heavens, you are there; if I make my bed in the depths, you are there. If I rise on the wings of the dawn, if I settle on the far side of the sea, even there your hand will guide me, your right hand will hold me fast.'

Such love was overwhelming. And when I looked at Phil, propped against the pillows, I knew that he felt likewise.

Derek's choice of Scripture was from Isaiah 40:27 to 41:29, and spoke of God's healing power – in this life and the next.

'But those who hope in the Lord will renew their strength. They will soar on wings like eagles; they will run and not grow weary, they will walk and not be faint.'

When I went home that night, I lay alone in my big double bed, staring into the darkness and trying to analyse my confusion.

First, was the fact that I was certainly not the only person praying for Phil's healing. Even if my faith was inadequate, I couldn't believe that that was true of everyone else. Nor, from my understanding of God – especially through His dealings with Job – did I believe that He was capable of making a mistake, or allowing His purposes to be thwarted by our limitations.

There had been a time when I had wondered if my prayers for Phil's healing had come to nought because of some unconfessed sin in my life and I recalled an occasion, quite recently, when Phil had shared a similar experience with me.

'When I was first diagnosed HIV positive,' he'd said, 'I had to grapple with the thought that it was, perhaps, a punishment from God for some wrongdoing or other.'

I'd looked at him quizzically and he'd continued, 'I have been less than honest with you about something . . . '

He'd refused to be drawn, except to say that he had told his father of the situation. 'Dad reassured me,' Phil had said. 'He told me that no matter what I had done, God was not an avenging God who sent punishment on His people. On the contrary, he said, He was a God of love who sent His only Son precisely so that He could take all punishment on Himself.'

We had never read Joni Eareckson's testimony of her own disability, in which she had admitted to the same feelings of guilt, but Mum and Dad had given us a copy of *Secret Strength*, the daily reading guide that Joni had written, and both Phil and I had benefited greatly from her insights.

At Phil's request I had bought a copy of David Watson's book, *Fear No Evil* and had read of his belief that God can go on working in a life and bring about healing, in spite of medical evidence to the contrary. It was a comforting thought. Nevertheless, it was simply no good pretending that I could conjure up a faith that I did not possess. Although I never doubted God's healing power, I still could not believe that Phil would be cured on earth.

One thing I did know, however, and I knew it with an absolute certainty: Phil's frail and weakened body would

be restored to wholeness and health in eternity. And with
that peaceable thought, I slept, at last.

Next morning, as I poured Ready Brek into Natasha's
breakfast bowl, I attempted to summarise my feelings.

'One day,' I said to her, 'Daddy will have a new body. A
strong, healthy body. With strong healthy legs. And when
he's in heaven, he'll be able to run and jump and do all
the things he's too sick to do now.'

Carefully, her spoon poised at the ready and her head
on one side, she considered my statement. 'Would he be
able to chase me round the garden, like Grandpa does?'
she asked.

'Yes, honey, he would,' I replied, 'except that he'll be
with Jesus and you'll be with me.' And I smoothed the
silky curtain of white-blonde hair from her eyes and urged
her to eat up her cereal.

If I'd ever doubted her capacity for understanding, my
uncertainty was soon to be confounded. Sometime later,
I overheard her telling a little friend, Ben, that her
Daddy was going to have a 'lubbly new body, in heaven
with Jesus'.

*   *   *

After his colostomy, Phil was able to eat again, though
he still took Meritene as additional protein. With the
consequent gain in weight – two kilos by the end of
the month – came increased strength and endurance. He
began to want to go into work again, rather than stay in
bed and, when his sense of humour returned as well, he
became more like his old self. Now that his sleep was no
longer disturbed by the necessity of using the pot at night,
I moved back from the spare room and joined him in our
own bedroom.

With many of the problems of evacuation resolved,
now that Phil was fitted with a *poche*, we discovered
difficulties of a different sort. One day, we sat in the
sunshine beside the lake at Hermance oblivious of the

fact that the bag was dangerously full. Suddenly, it burst, forcing the clip off and distributing its malodorous contents with embarrassing abandon. Red-faced, we vowed never to be caught out like that again.

In the meantime, with his 'guts' now largely sorted out, Phil found that other things began to bother him. The previous autumn he'd had a couple of tumbles and, despite the shots that he'd given himself at the time, had suffered pain in his left knee ever since. The discomfort was exacerbated by his enforced inactivity and, increasingly, he found himself less able to straighten his leg. It seemed set at an angle of 45°.

The orthopaedic doctor whom we saw explained why.

'The tendons and muscles have shortened, due to lack of exercise. They just won't stretch any more,' he said, and he gave Phil some simple exercises to do.

When we left, Phil said, half-joking, half-serious: 'One day, if I ever get through this, I'll have a plastic knee joint.' From then on, he hung on to that as a hope for the future.

Despite his disappointment and disability, however, he managed to help with the games at Natasha's party for her fourth birthday on 12th May. It was good, too, to see him fit enough to lead the Bible study group that we occasionally hosted at the flat.

Then one day, towards the end of the month, Phil's intestines popped out of the incision made for his colostomy. With some difficulty, he managed to push everything back in again. But when the same thing occurred the following day, and no amount of pushing would keep it in, I took him back to the Hôpital Cantonal. How frustrated he was when they kept him in for a few nights, especially when Mark, his best friend from university days, came to visit us from England, with his wife Anne and their son Joe.

Within a day or two, however, Phil was allowed home and, whilst Joe and Natasha amused themselves happily together, the four of us played Trivial Pursuit. For all the world like normal, fun-loving adults, I thought to myself – and I tried not to be too disappointed when several days of playing host to our guests inevitably took their toll upon Phil's strength and endurance. Finally, after a trip up the Salève in the *téléphérique*, we saw our visitors off at the station. When we returned home, Phil admitted to his fatigue.

'I just don't feel I can push myself any more,' he said, and subsided on to the settee.

For the next fortnight, he endeavoured to keep going into work, despite the fact that his intestines were continually popping out, causing him considerable pain. Once again, his appetite began to diminish and by the time we went to Crêt-Bérard on the church retreat at the beginning of June, he was showing great signs of strain. Even so, on the Saturday night, we presented a musical quiz together, with me playing my clarinet and Phil acting as compère. It was a huge success and we couldn't help but reflect, as we went to bed that night, that the theme of the retreat was pertinent to us: Knowing God's Will. It seemed to me that Jesus had promised us life abundant and that, in keeping with His will, that was exactly what we were experiencing!

What I had not appreciated, was that Phil's colostomy was only partial, in that the end of his intestine had been sewn to the abdominal wall for evacuation. 10th June was his next scheduled hospital visit and, in view of the problems that had occurred, it was decided to operate further, to complete the surgery already begun.

For nearly a week – during which Natasha developed a cough that prevented us visiting every day – the operation was delayed. Finally, it went ahead successfully, though Phil, with the added inconvenience of a shared room, was in a good deal of pain afterwards. Again, he felt unable to eat and anxiously, he fretted.

'Honey, we don't have it so bad,' I said, to encourage him, and I cited some friends who had telephoned to tell e of their marital difficulties.

Humbly, he acknowledged the extent of our good fortune in that respect. 'You're right. The Bible study we've just done in Daniel, when the three men were put in the fiery furnace, is a perfect example of God's faithfulness. If they could trust Him to see them through their circumstances, then so can I.'

Eventually, about a week after the operation, he greeted me with the news he'd been waiting for.

'They think I can come home on Monday,' he said, hopefully.

In the event, however, a high temperature prevented his release and he was put on a drip. What had begun as a hard week, turned into a difficult fortnight: the following day, on my way to the hospital, I had my wallet stolen.

It seemed that the problems were mounting up and even my implacable façade began to show signs of wear. After reporting the theft to the police, I rushed around in an attempt to make up lost time, only to find, when we finally made it to the hospital, that the ward doctors had just begun their rounds. Forced to wait whilst they examined Phil, I was overwhelmed by a sense of injustice after all my effort. I burst into tears.

Sinking on to a grey plastic chair in the ante room, I wept profusely, whilst Natasha watched, mystified. Through my sobs I tried to explain and she eventually sidled up, put her arms around my neck, and cuddled me as best she could.

'They only doin' their job, Mummy,' she said, adopting the soothing tones she'd so often heard me use. And oddly enough, I found her attitude very comforting.

*   *   *

That was not always the case, however, as I told Simonne a few days later.

'I'm worried about Tash,' I said.

We had crossed the border for a shopping expedition in Annemasse. Food in the French hypermarkets was cheaper than in Switzerland and a trip such as this was a frequent event – usually whilst the children were at school.

'Oh? Why's that?' Simonne asked, scooping up baby Joseph, and seating him in the front of her shopping trolley.

'She never stops whining and running away at the hospital,' I replied. 'She's become thoroughly unco-operative lately. I don't know whether her acting-up is part of normal childhood – or because her life has been one long round of hospital visits.'

Slowly, we made our way between the aisles, selecting packets of foodstuffs and mentally comparing prices with those of Geneva.

'It's probably just a phase,' Simonne said, to soothe me.

I shook my head. 'I don't think so,' I said.

We had arrived at the freezer and chilled-food section and for a few moments were intent upon loading our trolleys with meat. It was a taxing task, requiring all our attention as there was a limit on what we were allowed to take over the border without being obliged to declare it at Customs. Eventually, we moved on, free to resume our conversation once more.

'She just isn't having a normal life,' I continued. 'She's been going to the hospital since she was a month old. And in the past three weeks she's been with me to visit Phil almost every day.'

Simonne looked surprised.

'Oh – a couple of times someone from church has had her. Or one of the *benevoles* has taken her out. But most of the time it's been a half-hour ride on the tram, followed by another on the bus then a couple of hours stuck in a hospital ward. It's so confining for a child. I've tried to make it fun by breaking our journey sometimes, to stop off at McDonalds . . . '

' . . . Her favourite restaurant,' Simonne grinned, as we joined the queue at the checkout.

' . . . and sometimes we've had a Coke at the hos-ital . . . '

' . . . Her favourite drink . . . '

I laughed, in spite of myself. 'Right! But I worry. Is she going to look back on her childhood with resentment? There have been times when she's said she didn't want to go and see Daddy . . . '

Simonne paused in the act of taking a bag of French *crépes* from her trolley. 'But she's been fine when you've got there, hasn't she?' she said. 'Honestly, Jana, I don't know what you're worrying about. Children are pretty resilient.'

I pursed my lips, not entirely convinced. 'I suppose she plays with her toys at the hospital as well as she would at home . . . ' I said, doubtfully.

'Of course she does,' Simonne responded. 'And now you've taken the TV and video in for Phil, she's in her element watching the Turtles, isn't she?'

I smiled and nodded. She was probably right. Tash had as healthy an interest in childish things as any other youngster.

'She keeps talking about Shredder in the same vein as the Lord Jesus,' I said. 'I'll have to watch that she doesn't get her theology thoroughly muddled up . . . '

*   *   *

Still, the whole question of Natasha nagged in the back of my mind and the next time I saw Ruth, our *benevole*, I asked her views.

'I'm concerned about what she thinks of her daddy,' I said.

Ruth smiled, reassuringly. 'I shouldn't worry, Jana. Tash talks quite naturally about Phil when I take her out. Now and then she'll say things like "my daddy isn't like Steve, because he can't walk," but I think she accepts it as quite normal. Different – but normal.'

'I do try to talk to her about him,' I said. 'I tell her that we must look after Daddy because he's sick. And I ask her questions to help her make a picture of him in her mind

Things like "what does Daddy look like?" and "what does Daddy do?"'

Sometimes I wondered if she felt neglected because of Phil's illnesses and I'd tell her that 'no other daddy loves you like he does'. However, I had never told her that he had an illness from which there was no recovery. I felt that she was too young to know that.

It was heartening to hear that friends like Simonne, Ruth and Francesco cared about Natasha and her understanding of the situation, and were actively involved in encouraging her to express herself. Over the months, we had come to know our *benevoles* quite well and appreciated their sensitivity and insight.

One evening, when Ruth was preparing to leave the flat, after sitting with Tasha whilst I had been out, she dropped something on the floor. In an instant, it slid across the polished parquet and disappeared under the settee. Ruth cursed.

'I'm so sorry,' she said immediately, a flush appearing beneath her olive complexion. 'I didn't mean to offend you. I don't go to church, you see . . . '

Somehow I found myself mentioning, quite naturally, that Phil and I were working on a book, expressing our faith in the face of his disease. Ruth was intrigued. Instead of going home immediately, as she'd intended, she sat down again on the settee.

'You see, we know that Phil will be going to heaven,' I said, my natural diffidence forgotten in my enthusiasm to share with her. 'When he dies, it will only be his body that goes in the grave. A shell. The essential part of him – his soul – will live on.'

'But aren't you afraid for the future?' Ruth asked.

I seated myself on a dining-chair and considered her question. Behind me, through the french windows that opened on to the balcony, traffic sounds floated in on the soft evening air.

'There have been times when it's been scary,' I said, honestly. 'But when you contrast his wasted body and all the pain he's suffering now, with the wonderful eternity he'll enjoy in heaven – it makes it easier to bear.'

In the lamplight, Ruth's dark eyes shone with sympathy. 'But you'll miss him?' she asked.

I nodded. 'Of course. And he doesn't want to leave us. But we know we'll meet again . . . '

Memories flooded back into my mind. The day that Phil had said that he felt he couldn't go on much longer, I had asked if he would be my guardian angel. I still had no idea what contact – if any – there might be between those in this world and the next. But Phil had looked at me with such love and understanding – and whatever he had believed himself, he'd not said anything to make me feel silly. He'd simply said: 'I will, if I can.' And I'd felt at peace and had wasted no more time worrying.

' . . . In heaven?' Ruth asked, fumbling with her coat. 'You'll be together again in heaven?'

Again I nodded. Then I stood up and pushed my chair under the table.

'But the most important thing,' I finished, as Ruth rose to go, 'is that Phil will be with Jesus. You see, being a Christian is not a religion. It's a relationship.'

*　　　*　　　*

If I'd stopped to think, I'd have realised that it was probably just as well that being a Christian didn't require one to adhere to a set pattern of behaviour. Like it or not, Phil and I succumbed to a whole range of different emotions and could only come to the Father as we were. Our security lay in the knowledge that, just as I had never stopped loving Tash, no matter how undesirable her conduct, no more would God, when we fell short of Jesus' perfect example. 'If we claim to be without sin, we deceive ourselves and the truth is not in us. If we confess our sins, he is faithful and just and will forgive us our sins and purify us from all unrighteousness.' 1 John 1:9.

The 29th June was hot and sultry with a yellowish haze

that hung heavily over the lake, as I made my way to the hospital. Saturday morning shoppers jostled on the pavements and crowded on to buses and trams, leaving me no alternative but to strap-hang. Every time we stopped to let passengers off and on, I clutched Tash's hand in mine to prevent her being swept away in the surge, and again when we fought our way to the door at our stop. By the time we'd walked to the hospital, packed into the lift and haltingly progressed to the third floor, I felt suffocated and exhausted.

The moment I saw Phil, I knew that the news was bad. The previous evening he had been subjected to an ultrasound scan, and I guessed that he must have learned the results. Anxiously, I approached his bed.

'You've heard?' I asked, without preamble.

He nodded. 'This morning . . . '

'Well?' I pulled up a chair and sat, ignoring Tash, who played on the floor.

'They've found some lumps on my liver.' His tone was flat and his face wan with the effort of his battle to get well.

My heart sank. 'What sort of lumps?' I asked, keeping my voice low so as not to disturb his room-mate.

Phil shrugged. 'They think it's the same sort of thing that was forming the obstruction in my intestines,' he replied.

I sat back and relaxed. 'Well, you don't need to worry, then,' I said, more cheerfully. 'They'll be able to cut them out.'

Phil hesitated. 'Actually,' he said at length, 'the surgeon says they won't do anything . . . '

The man in the other bed stirred fretfully in his sleep and I glanced at him, waited until he had settled, then lowered my voice again.

'Why not?' I whispered, and grasped hold of Phil's thin hand where it lay on top of the sheet.

Again he hesitated. In the harsh morning light, his face looked more drawn than ever, etched with deep shadows that I didn't remember seeing before. Behind the gold-rimmed glasses, his eyes were unfocused – a pale, vacuous blue. With an effort, he drew his attention back to me.

'They won't do anything,' he said at last, 'because . . . there really isn't any point . . . '

I stared at him for several moments – uncomprehending – dazzled by the sun's rays glinting off the window. I could think of absolutely nothing to say. After all this time of waiting and wondering – expecting the worst and hoping for the best – there seemed to be no relevant words.

Haltingly, Phil summed up the situation: 'Look at my life: my body's no longer under my control; I've virtually no response in my legs and back; I can't even make love to you any more. Not only do I lack the physical ability, I've been robbed of the mental desire as well. The whole sexual aspect of our marriage has been removed . . . It feels as if my masculinity has been ripped away.' His voice wavered and tears filled my eyes. 'As if that's not enough,' he continued doggedly, 'because of the constant pain I'm in, I can't even hug you or kiss you as I'd like to. What's the point? What's it all about?

'I keep hanging on. Thinking that one day a cure will be found. Wanting to get better . . . Wanting to see Tash grow up . . . And to grow old with you . . . but instead of improving, other things happen to make me sicker.'

Feebly, he turned on his back and lay staring at the ceiling.

'That's the horrible thing about this disease,' he said – so softly that I could barely hear. 'There's no cure. And there's no remission . . . '

*   *   *

I was unable to shake off the depression that took a hold of me, and all that evening I felt engulfed in grief. Even my homespun philosophy of busyness failed to lift my mood, and the chocolate cake that I made for the fellowship group barbecue the following afternoon, sank in the middle. As

I took it from the oven and contemplated its sorry state, I couldn't help feeling that it was an apt reflection of my own sentiments. Flat and sad.

Why is it that everything seems to go wrong all at once, I thought, with a sense of defeat? And from the quarry-tiled floor and hard, uncompromising walls of the kitchen, the clatter of cooking utensils resounded with a hollow echo – a voice of desolation.

Even as I allowed the thought to enter my head, another followed fast on its heels. Paulette had told me, when Phil had been so desperately ill prior to our departure for Geneva, of a truth she'd learned when baby James had died. 'When you hit rock bottom,' she'd said, 'remember that the rock beneath you is Jesus'. I was not alone. Nor was I defeated. Jesus had experienced much the same temptation during His days in the wilderness. Yet He had drawn on the strength of God, the Father, to avert any tendency to self-pity. So, too, could I.

Squaring my shoulders, I lifted down the icing sugar, and prepared to disguise the sunken cake.

I'll take it anyway, I thought defiantly, and say I sculpted it to look like the Alps.

After all, Phil would be home tomorrow. And he would need me to be strong.

Besides, I didn't want to waste eight eggs!

*   *   *

Phil was finally allowed home on the last day of June and we were able to go straight from the hospital to the fellowship barbecue, though we did not stay long. He now had two incisions in his abdomen, and two *poches*. Throughout the following days, he sat under a great cloud of depression and pain.

'I feel lousy,' he said, when I took him breakfast in bed. 'It's so frustrating not to be able to control my bodily functions.'

'What do you mean?' I asked, with alarm.

'Oh, my bowels are okay,' Phil said, guessing my meaning. 'But now I seem to have lost control of my bladder.'

The urge to pass water had become so acute that he would sit with a urinal beside him all day. About once an hour, his muscles would contract involuntarily, and he'd grab at the bottle in an attempt to avert an accident. Frequently, he was too late.

An even greater frustration to him, however, was the complete loss of feeling in both legs. The muscles and tendons were utterly inflexible. No longer able to straighten his left knee beyond an angle of 90°, he was quite unable to use his crutches to get about the flat.

'It's very painful,' he admitted. 'It throbs, all the time, non-stop. I dread doing anything where movement is concerned.'

Reduced to such a state of incapacity, Phil could no longer dress himself and even turning over in bed at night was torture. Early in our marriage he had told me how his mother and sisters used to run their fingers gently over his swollen joints when he'd been a child, because the tickling sensation had soothed the pain. Now, whenever I was not otherwise occupied, he begged me to do likewise, and it was obvious that this simple action gave him some relief.

Morphine, however, was the only real solution. Phil had been taking such medication in liquid or tablet form since March and much as I hated having him use it, there was no alternative but for me to fetch him a prescription from the hospital.

I told Phil's mum, next time she rang.

'I'm afraid morphine's always been a sign of the beginning of the end,' she said, confirming my own thoughts.

Watching TV movies and videos was one of the few hobbies still left to Phil, and he clung to this simple pleasure, with all the fervour he could muster. Though heavily sedated, he managed to rally when Ruth Jones, our *benevole*, suggested one day that she take him to the cinema to see *Jungle Fever*, whilst I prepared for the arrival of friends from New York City.

Later, when he and Ruth returned, the six of us dined outdoors at the Pizza Borgia – though Phil got a very sore bum from sitting so long.

'Never mind,' I said, rubbing him later to restore his circulation, 'according to Ruth, we can order a special Roho cushion for you. It's very expensive, but it'll make sitting more comfortable.'

He would need that, I thought. Before we set off for France, to join his family on holiday, later in the week.

9

And a Time to Let Go

*'I know that my Redeemer lives, and that in the
end He will stand upon the earth. And after my
skin has been destroyed, yet in my flesh I will
see God.'*

Job 19:25, 26

'How long d'you think it'll take us, hon?'

I looked up from the maps I was studying and across the
living-room to Phil. He lay on the sofa, engrossed in a film
on TV. He wore a T-shirt, baggy grey jogging pants, and
his usual basketball boots – high on the ankle to support
and protect the joints. Beneath the clothing, his arms were
like sticks and his body skeletal. He looked like a victim
of Belsen.

It grieved me to see him. In this last week of July there
had been a subtle deterioration in his faculties. The heat
didn't help.

'How long, hon?' I asked again. I hoped that by
involving him in the navigation of our trip to France,
he might feel of some use.

Slowly, with all the deliberation of an invalid who has
become unpractised in drawing conclusions or making
decisions, Phil considered my question.

'I should think . . . about . . . three hours,' he said, at
last.

I frowned, surprised. 'Three hours? Is that all?'

He nodded. 'It's not far.'

I looked again at the map. The distances didn't look too great. And the roads were good. Doubtfully, I conceded. Perhaps he was right.

I changed tack. 'You have packed all your medication, haven't you?'

Phil nodded again. His attention was glued to the TV screen.

'I left a bag on the bed,' I persisted. 'Did you put everything in?'

'Yes,' he said. 'It's all there.'

Phil had always been fanatical about making sure that he had the right medication and enough of it – especially when he was ill. In view of his diminished mobility, I felt that it was good for him to know that I trusted him still. If there was one thing that the conference in Crêt-Bérard had taught me, it was that people who are sick need to feel in control over some aspect of their lives: to assert a degree of independence.

I checked quickly down my list. Satisfied that all was complete, I gathered together the various documents on the table, and shoved them into my bag.

'Right. We're ready, then.'

I hauled the last suitcase downstairs, into the car boot. The wheelchair was next and when that was stowed away, I returned for Phil. I knew, from past experience, that the pressure of my arms under his back and knees caused him excruciating pain. Carefully, I eased him from the sofa. Then I lifted him like a baby.

It was a practised technique and he weighed barely eighty-five pounds. Nevertheless, it was no easy matter to carry him down the winding stone steps to the street. Unfailingly, I always managed to bump some part of his anatomy on wall or door jamb. It was an effort, too, to get Tash to co-operate, to hold the heavy outer door open ong enough for us to pass through. Frequently, by the ae I had deposited Phil in the rear of the car where he could stretch out, I was feeling the strain. That morning was no exception.

'*Mais vous êtes vraiment forte, madame.*' I looked up and smiled my thanks. The remark came from the woman who worked in the art gallery, next door to the *patisserie*. Despite my fatigue, I felt a surge of pride. It flattered my ego to be admired for my stamina and inwardly I patted myself on the back.

Then I recalled: when I'd first learned to cope with Phil's wheelchair, I'd been full of myself. Yet every time I'd gloried in my own strength and achievement, someone would come up to me from church and say: 'I've been praying for you specially this week.' Chastened and repentant, I'd be reminded that it was not my strength, but God's that had seen me through. It was He who had kept me going, physically, mentally and emotionally. His strength was made perfect in my weakness.

Humbled and contrite with the memory, I turned back to Phil.

'It's a shame that cushion hasn't arrived,' I remarked, matter-of-factly as I belted him in, then watched Tash climb into her car seat beside him. 'You could have done with that for the journey.'

'It's not far.' He spread the map on his lap. 'I'll be okay.'

I buckled Natasha's restraint, made myself comfortable behind the steering wheel, then set off.

'This is gonna be fun,' I said, cheerfully, as I headed the car towards the autoroute. 'Three hours? We'll be there by lunch.'

*　　*　　*

It was almost dusk when we arrived at the villa Mum and Dad had rented in Les Issambres. Weary and dishevelled, I pulled up before the house and took in the scene. It was beautiful: a large airy building set into a hillside, with private pool below, surrounded by tall leafy trees. The noted, with dismay, the steep stone steps that gave access to both. Hopeless for a wheelchair, I thought.

Mum greeted us, emerging from the lamplit house and exclaiming, 'Wasn't it hard to find! We thought we'd never get here.'

She took charge of Tash who, loosed from the car, was filled with a boisterous excitement. Then Dad helped me to get Phil into the house and on to the sofa.

'Phil's not feeling very well,' I told Mum, once I'd settled him comfortably.

'It's probably only the journey, Jana. How long did it take?'

'About eight hours, I think.'

'Eight?' Dad paused in the process of bringing in my luggage. 'That seems excessive!'

'Right!' I glanced at Phil. I didn't like talking about him as if he were not there. Somehow, I felt that it robbed him of dignity. However, he was in no fit state to answer.

'I let Phil navigate,' I said brightly, endeavouring to make light of the matter. 'And we went miles out of our way. I reckon getting lost accounted for at least an hour extra.'

In fact, Phil's estimate of three hours for the journey had been grossly inaccurate. Although I didn't like casting aspersions on his judgement, I had found his opinion hard to credit and had checked *en route* when we'd stopped for petrol; seven hours had been nearer the mark.

I mentioned none of this to Phil's parents. There was no point in worrying them. For some time, Phil's greatest fear had been that an AIDS-related dementia would set in, causing gradual atrophy of the brain, impaired memory and reasoning processes and even, possibly, changes in personality. In the light of recent events, I was increasingly concerned for the future. At the same time, I was grateful that Phil's mental faculties had remained undiminished for so long. Silently, I thanked God for His care.

*   *   *

By the time Mum had prepared a simple meal, Phil was fit enough to join the family at the table, and conversation over dinner was all to do with God's grace in our time of need.

'It's wonderfully uplifting to have so many people praying for you,' I said. 'People from our church in Geneva; our families, of course; and friends in America and in England.'

We'd heard that our fellowship group at St Aldate's in Oxford met regularly to intercede on our behalf. What amazed me, however, was the friends of friends, or families of friends – folk who had never met us – who regularly remembered us in prayer.

'Steve Arkinstall's parents' church in Surrey pray for us every week,' I said, taking a large piece of crusty French bread from the basket that Dad offered me.

'And Liz Goosey's mother's church in Birmingham,' Phil reminded me. Phil had been best man at Liz's wedding when she had married his university friend, Mick.

'I don't believe we could have got this far without the support we've received,' I said.

Tash prayed that night, as she had done every night since April, when we had told her of the holiday villa and pool: 'Dear Jesus, please make my Daddy be well enuff to go in de swimming pool wiv me.'

Phil's doctors had said, in Tasha's hearing, that they thought he would be well enough to bathe, complete with his *poches*. I had mentioned it to Mum on the phone and neither she nor I were at all keen on the idea, in case a leak should develop in the bags and allow the potentially infectious contents to seep out and contaminate the pool. There was such childlike trust in Tash's prayerful request and, knowing that in this instance the desires of her heart could not be met, my eyes filled with tears.

'I'm sure Daddy will be able to paddle his legs in the water when you're swimming, even if he can't go in with you,' I said and, smoothing her silky blonde hair on the pillow, I kissed her goodnight.

The following day, after attempting to eat pâté at lunchtime, Phil was very sick.

'I'm trying to get him to eat,' Mum said, all her nursery training coming to the fore. 'He's so thin.'

'Yeah,' I agreed, with concern. 'But I think he finds the Meritene easier to digest.'

If only I could ensure that he had four bottles a day, I thought, then at two hundred and fifty calories each, he would at least be receiving some nourishment. Determinedly, I set about increasing Phil's intake.

But it seemed that my efforts were in vain. Next morning, when he woke, Phil was vague and disoriented and only rallied when we hauled him down the steps and seated him on the edge of the pool with his feet in the water.

At the end of the week, Trina and I took a trip to Cannes with Phil. It proved altogether too tiring for him and we decided to leave him in his wheelchair with an ice-cream and a book whilst we went off shopping without him. Later, when we all returned to the villa, it was obvious to the family that the day's outing had been far too strenuous for him. From then on, I had to go exploring on my own or with Trina, grateful that Mum and Dad were there to relieve me of some of the responsibilities of looking after an active four-year-old and a very sick husband. I was determined to have a good time. I knew what lay ahead!

Throughout the final week of our holiday, Phil spent each day reclining on a portable bed on the upper balcony, because sitting for too long made his bum sore. He was uncomfortable, too, because of the intense heat. No matter how often we changed him, the sweaty incontinency pads chafed at his skin. Each day, he seemed to decline visibly, had no interest in the newspaper, and would only speak when spoken to. When he did say something, it made no sense and he didn't seem to be 'all there'. Sadly I acknowledged the advance of the dementia he had dreaded.

Eventually, I spoke to Mum of my concern. 'His hands are terribly shaky. And he seems to think if I go out anywhere that I'm going to be away overnight. I don't know whether it's just the effects of the morphine, or whether the virus is affecting his brain.'

Whatever it was, we agreed that Phil wasn't Phil any more.

'I've read articles by the spouses of people with Alzheimer's disease,' I continued. 'They say that the person they've loved and lived with for so many years just isn't there . . . That's how I feel about Phil.'

Watching the man I loved slowly disappearing filled me with an infinite sorrow. Phil was such a wonderful person. Already I missed his opinions and his help in a variety of ways. Most of all, I missed his sense of humour and with it, the chance of being able to be silly with him. I was sad, too, for Natasha. Her dad would never be able to have fun with her the way he would have liked to. Silently, I wondered how much time Phil had left.

The registration forms for a conference in Copenhagen in June '92 had arrived just before we'd left home. I told Dad. 'Phil was invited to be a speaker for the first time. It would be nice if he could – but I don't know if he'll be around that long.' Sadly I reflected. It seemed strange to be thinking of plans for a future in which Phil might no longer be a part.

Unaware of what he was doing, Phil began behaving like a child, blowing his nose on his T-shirt and emptying his *poche* anywhere and everywhere. There seemed to be no end to the cleaning up and running around after him, and we were constantly washing bedding and clothing. Then, only a week into the holiday, I discovered that I had been wrong to entrust him with the packing of all his medical stuff. He had evidently not been capable, and had brought nothing like enough Fluconazol – the medication he took regularly to combat yeast infections. We were short of *poches* too. The heat caused Phil to sweat more and as this loosened the tape that secured the bags to his body, I had no option but to change them more frequently than I had anticipated.

The shortage of *poches* was easily remedied by a trip to the nearest *pharmacie*. Replenishing the missing drug, however, was another matter. Normally available to Phil on prescription, it would have been prohibitively expensive to buy over the counter. And because AIDS was exempted from all travel and health insurances, we had no cover. Praying hard, I held my breath and hoped that, in the absence of his pills, Phil would not develop thrush before we returned home.

One evening, as I was settling Phil into bed for the night, he complained of a loss of sensation in his left hand.

'It feels completely numb.' He pinched the skin to demonstrate.

My heart sank as my mind went back to the Christmas of 1989, when he had experienced numbness of his feet. The uncertainty and anxiety had been unbearable.

'Is it similar to what happened to your feet?' I asked.

If so, I wasn't sure that I could cope. A loss of dexterity would presage untold problems: he would no longer be able to hold his bottle of Meritene, his wee bottle, or a book.

Normally, if something was bothering Phil, I had the reassurance of knowing that I could call Dr Hirschel. With typical scientific curiosity, Phil liked to have details of his ailments and to know the reason for their development, though he was always loth to bother the doctors himself. I had no such reticence. Now, however, we were far from home and that was not possible.

Fortunately, Phil never mentioned his hands again. However, worse was to follow. On the last evening of our holiday, as I was packing to go home, I noticed that the waste in his *poche* was bloody.

'Looks like you've got a bleed, honey,' I said. 'You'd better give yourself a shot.'

I rummaged in the bag that I'd packed and found the necessary items. Then I broke open a bottle of Factor VIII, filled the syringe and passed it to Phil. He was sitting in his wheelchair, staring vacantly, and his fingers trembled as he took the instrument.

'Phil!' I put my hand over his and tightened his grip. Then with mounting alarm, I watched his attempts to inject himself. He seemed unable to focus properly, or to hold the hypodermic steady. For the first time ever, he appeared to lack the strength to push the needle into a vein. After some moments, he gave up the struggle.

Frantic with worry, I rushed into the living-room to tell Mum but though she and Patrina followed me back into the bedroom, neither was able to deliver the shot.

'What are we going to do?' I asked. 'I can't take him home like this tomorrow.'

With frightening clarity, it suddenly dawned upon me just how vulnerable we were. I was a woman in a foreign country, with a small dependent daughter and a sick husband. All too easily, I succumbed to my fears. Bereft of medical support, I had been looking to Mum and Dad to know what to do and had overlooked the fact that they seemed to be looking to me. Now I realised that as Phil's wife, it was I who had ultimate responsibility. For an instant my mind froze.

Then I took stock. God was in control! No matter what happened, He had promised never to forsake those whom He loved. Spiritually, mentally and emotionally, I drew a deep breath. Panic would be self-defeating. Instinctively I knew that my terrors had to be faced and addressed if ever they were to be dissolved. There was only one way forward. I had to discover for myself the necessary course of action, then put it into practice.

To begin with, I tried to contact a local doctor or nurse in Les Issambres. When that met with no success, Dad had a suggestion.

'Why don't we find a public phone and ring the local hospital to see if they can help?'

'That sounds like a good idea,' I said and put in a call to the hospital in Fréjus. To my profound relief, learned that the staff in *Urgences* would be able to give Phil his shot.

Between us, we managed to carry Phil out of the house, down the steps and into the car. Dad drove while I tried to navigate from the instructions I'd received over the phone. They were not very clear and eventually, after touring around for some time, we had to admit defeat and ask the way. My heart thumped wildly and I felt sick and dizzy with apprehension.

At last, we arrived. The instant I handed Phil over into the care of the doctor with whom I had spoken on the phone, my fears dissolved. It was so good to know that the situation was under the control of trained medical staff!

'*Votre mari a besoin d'une piqûre?*' a nurse asked, kindly.

I nodded. 'I've brought some *poches* and four bottles of Factor VIII,' I explained in French.

Whilst they changed Phil's bags and gave him his injection, I filled in the medical forms and chatted with the hospital doctor. His tenor, and that of the nurses, was of sympathy and compassion with no hint of distaste or condemnation at the sight of Phil's emaciated body. In the end, the whole episode had been dealt with relatively easily.

'Thank you, Lord,' I whispered as we made our way back to the villa.

* * *

It was two-thirty in the morning before we finally got to bed. I'd worried that I might not be alert enough to drive home next day and was grateful when Mum and Dad had insisted on accompanying me to Geneva, before making their own way back to England.

'It's all decided,' Mum said, in her no-nonsense voice. 'Trina can come with you to share the driving, then Phil can stretch out on the back seat of our car.'

We arrived back at the flat on Tuesday, 30th July and

I immediately rang Dr Hirschel to make an appointment for Phil to see him the following day, after Mum, Dad and Trina had left.

Lines of pain were etched on Phil's face as I carried him downstairs next morning and lifted him into the car. We dropped Natasha off with Simonne then went on to the hospital, and up to Dr Hirschel's consulting room on the second floor of the *Policlinique du Médecin*. Phil's colour was not good and he slumped in his wheelchair, silent and vacant.

'It's hard getting him to do much of anything these days,' I said. 'I have to talk to him like he's a child.'

Dr Hirschel nodded, gravely. 'And how are you coping in practical terms?'

'Getting him into bed isn't easy,' I admitted. 'He's such a dead-weight.'

The doctor scribbled something on a note pad then said, 'I am going to make an appointment with Social Services for you. They should be able to offer some practical help and advice.' He swivelled round, pulled himself forward on his chair so that he was looking up into Phil's face and spoke directly to him. 'I am going to take some blood tests,' he said. 'Then we'll see about renewing your pentamadine spray.'

The inhalant was a replacement for the Septrin that Phil had been taking ever since his attack of pneumocystis. Instead of three pills taken four times daily, he now inhaled – with constant urging from me to keep the tube in his mouth – for fifteen minutes once a month.

I glanced at Phil. His eyes were closed. 'He's not with it at all, is he, Doctor?'

'Is he ever confused about who you are?'

'Oh, no. He always knows Tash and me. But sometimes – like now – he hardly seems to know where he is.'

'He does seem a little disorientated,' Dr Hirschel agreed and he leaned forward again, so that his face was close to Phil's, and asked, 'Do you know what day it is today?'

Without hesitation, Phil raised his wrist, consulted his watch and accurately read aloud the time and date. I had to laugh. It was such a surprise!

Dr Hirschel smiled and leaned back in his chair. After some moments he asked, 'How do you both feel about prolonging life?'

I was seated sideways on to the doctor's desk. For a moment, I turned my head away from him and studied Phil. He appeared not to have heard, and continued to stare at the floor.

Through the window behind him, a line of white cloud edged its way across the square of blue that was all that was visible of the sky. There had been no sign of a weather front earlier, when we'd arrived at the hospital, and idly, I wondered if rain was forecast. Then I dismissed the idea. Most probably, the clouds would have dissipated before the day was out.

I turned back and stared at the identification tag on Dr Hirschel's white coat. What would he be offering in terms of extension, I wondered? Days? Weeks? Months, perhaps? So? Phil might have a longer life. But of what quality, I asked myself. The outlook was as nebulous as the weather.

I raised my head and looked the doctor square in the eye.

'We're both quite clear about that,' I said. And my voice was perfectly steady. 'We don't believe in extending life by artificial means.'

*   *   *

The 1st of August was a Swiss National Day and as 1991 was the 700th anniversary of the Republic's confederation, it was particularly special. After a lazy day at home, I took Tash out in the early evening to see the parade. Crowds lined the streets to watch and to listen, for at every intersection, four men from the parade set up 'r Alpenhorns to play a few bars of what sounded like a hymn. The instruments were huge and made a deep, throaty note that delighted Tash.

Steadily, we wended our way to the *mairie* in Thônex, where food was being served from stalls set up on the cobbled square. I drank vegetable soup from a commemorative cup, followed by roast pork in gravy, and Tash had the only thing that she would eat – chips and Coke. In the grounds of the *mairie*, there were merry-go-rounds and side-stalls and as we ate, we watched various people trying their skill with a William Tell crossbow and target.

It was good to feel a part of the celebration, though I had more than a little misgiving about leaving Phil alone. Juggling my time between him and Tash was proving to be quite a feat. She was a healthy four-year-old who needed my attention in terms of exercise, entertainment and commuting to and from school. Phil, on the other hand, had become childlike himself and was entirely unpredictable. I was constantly worried about what he would get up to during my absence.

He no longer used the wee bottle and had completely lost control of his bladder. Sometimes, he would feel the urge to urinate and grab the nearest vessel, be it his Meritene container or a drinking glass. Night after night, I would find myself lying awake listening for the sound of him playing with his *poche* in his sleep. Occasionally, he would empty it in the bed and, despite the use of incontinency pads, and of plastic-backed sheets on the mattress, it was a messy and unpleasant business. I couldn't help feeling saddened and appalled at the loss of dignity being suffered by the man I loved.

Keeping him clean was a nightmare. The bathroom was only a short distance from our bedroom but the effort of getting Phil there was enormous. Then I had to lower him into a bath of warm water, soap him all over, and wash his hair. Lifting him out again and drying him required Herculean strength on my part, and it was hard to tell which of us was the more exhausted by the time we collapsed on to the bed.

An appointment had been made for Phil to have a blood transfusion at the hospital on the day following the parade. This was a Friday so, after making arrangements to collect him later in the day, I returned home with Natasha and spent the rest of the morning doing the washing and catching up on the housework. By the time I collected Phil from the hospital that evening, I was as well satisfied with my achievements as with his improved appearance.

My satisfaction was short lived, however, when Phil emptied his *poche* in the bed that night. 'Washday's not for another week!' I wailed, inwardly, as I stripped the bed.

Really, I hadn't a moment's peace of mind when Phil was out of my sight. And though I took Tash to church on the Sunday, I spent the whole service wondering what he would have got up to by the time I returned home.

I was due to see Social Services next morning at the *hôpital*, and I wasn't sure that I could stand the strain of leaving Phil again. Fortunately, when I rang Ruth she agreed to come in and sit with him.

At the Social Services office, I explained that I was having difficulty with the practical aspects of looking after Phil, and that Dr Hirschel felt that I needed help. There was a certain diffidence in my request, in that I was dubious about my right to State welfare. For one thing, I was young and fit and possessed of an underlying sense that I should be able to cope. I was also a stranger in a foreign country. And finally, though by no means insignificantly, my husband was suffering from a highly emotive disease!

When I discovered, therefore, that the staff were adamant about my need of assistance, my relief was profound. Quantifying and defining the nature of that need, however, proved a problem in itself.

'We can arrange for nurses to call regularly,' a kindly Swiss matron told me, 'if you can tell us exactly what you require.'

I thought hard. 'Basically, I want someone to help with ashing my husband,' I said, in French. 'And some-
with a medical background who could stay with

him – and perhaps not mind having Tash, too, sometimes.'

At one time, I had considered engaging a fulltime nurse but the prohibitive cost and sporadic need made this option impracticable. Vaguely, I now half-hoped for someone who could sit and watch over Phil in my absence and who would not be averse to changing his *poche* and cleaning up after him when necessary.

The provision of nurses to help with keeping Phil clear appeared to present no problem and arrangements were made for one to call the following day. My second request, however, met with no success.

Not altogether satisfied, I went on to see Dr de Moerloose at the Haemophilia Centre on the fourth floor. He shook my hand, then indicated a chair and waited for me to seat myself.

'Ah, yes,' he said, when I explained that I had come from Social Services. 'Dr Hirschel contacted me. He said you would require some help at home. What is your husband's condition now?'

'Phil's not capable of giving himself a shot of Factor any more,' I explained. 'I wondered if it would be possible for someone to call?'

'Of course – we can arrange something,' he said immediately. 'The doctors in the haemophilia department are not at liberty to make house calls. However, I will give you the telephone number of the *Association des Médecins*. You have only to ring – day or night – any time, and a doctor will come out to give your husband an injection.' He leaned back in his chair and pushed a pencil back and forth through his fingers, regarding me thoughtfully.

I said, 'Thank you. Dr Hirschel doesn't think it will be long now.'

Dr de Moerloose shook his head regretfully. 'There is an organisation called *Pro Infirmis* that helps people with handicaps. Would you like me to telephone them and ask them to call?'

'Please.'

He reached for the phone, dialled the number, then spoke rapidly in French. 'Tomorrow?' he asked, looking enquiringly at me.

An appointment was made, and the following day a Monsieur Stadelmann came to the flat. He was most helpful and not only arranged for the Red Cross nurses to call, but also informed me of several appliances which would make life easier – such as a special hoist to get Phil in and out of the bath. With all the support being organised, I felt quite overwhelmed!

Wednesday, 7th August was Emilie's fifth birthday so Natasha was invited to spend the day with the Arkinstalls. As soon as she left with Simonne, a nurse arrived from the Red Cross and enquired how she might help. I asked her to give Phil a wash.

Phil seemed incapable of taking much in and when the nurse had finished, I sat quietly watching videos with him in the bedroom. The contents of his *poche* were dark with blood and that afternoon, when Dr Hirschel called, he gave Phil a shot of Factor VIII. I made Phil comfortable in bed, then walked with the doctor to the living-room. He took the seat I offered and waited expectantly.

'I've never seen anyone die before,' I said nervously. 'I've no idea what to expect.'

Dr Hirschel regarded me, kindly. 'Most AIDS patients die in hospital,' he replied. 'Not many people can cope with death at home.'

Mentally and physically I stiffened my backbone, rising to meet the challenge. 'Phil's been in hospital so much this year . . . I know he'd rather be at home.'

'It is very hard . . . '

I gripped the chair arm. 'But if he went into hospital, I wouldn't be able to see much of him. Because of Tash. He might die without me being there.'

Dr Hirschel nodded. His face was filled with sympathy. 'I understand . . . ' he said.

Mollified, I relaxed.

'On the other hand,' I said, 'I wouldn't want Phil

to suffer unnecessarily, just so I could have him at home.'

For a few moments silence fell between us. I was seated at the table and, turning away from the doctor and the familiar room, I stared out of the window. The troughs of ivy-leafed geraniums that Tash and I had planted in the spring as tiny cuttings now streamed through the balcony rail, a profusion of scarlet, white and fuchsia pink. It was all very symbolic of the life force that was, even now, draining out of Phil.

Without turning my head, I asked, 'How much longer do you think Phil has?'

There was a slight pause and I looked quickly back at the doctor.

Instantly, he replied. 'Not long, I think. But then, when you first arrived in Geneva – what, two years ago? – Dr Wintsch, who saw your husband at the time, told me that she thought you would have to go back to England. She did not think that you would return to Switzerland. So you see! We doctors are not infallible!' He spread his large, capable hands in the air and his brown eyes crinkled at the corners.

I smiled.

Then Dr Hirschel went on, 'He seems more comfortable. But you know, you must not feel that you *have* to keep him at home.'

I nodded, but said nothing.

'It's up to you,' said the doctor, misinterpreting my silence. 'Play it by ear.'

But my mind was made up. I'd promised Phil that I wouldn't leave him; that I'd see him through to the end. And that was exactly what I intended to do.

*   *   *

That evening, Mike and Juliene Wallace came over to show their support.

'You can't come out for a meal with us,' Juliene said, 'so we're going to make one here for you.'

Mike and Juliene were one of several young American couples who attended the Evangelical Baptist Church of Geneva and, since joining our house group, they had become good friends. Mike was a chef, who had trained at the Culinary Institute of America in the US and now worked at the Ramada Rennaissance, whilst Juliene was a secretary at the United Nations.

Between the two of them they made a delicious pizza for us, and even Phil managed to eat a little. When they had gone, we agreed that we had greatly enjoyed their company and appreciated their love and concern.

'It's done us both good,' I said, as we went to bed.

The love of friends was a vital part of God's wonderful provision, as I reminded myself next day. Anxious to avert another catastrophe, I had lain awake for hours in the night, listening to Phil playing with his nappy and his *poche*. By morning, I was suffering from a marked lack of sleep.

When the Red Cross called to give him a bed-bath, later that day, I was more than grateful to have been relieved of the task. Still more so when Ruth called and offered to stay with Tash and Phil in the afternoon, so that I could go to see a movie. It was a comedy called *The Hard Way*. It seemed an apt title.

'It was great to get out,' I said, thankfully, on my return. 'There's nothing like a good laugh to release your tension.'

That night, I took a sleeping pill to stave off my anxiety and did not waken on the Friday morning until almost seven o'clock. For some moments, I lay listening. Phil's breathing sounded very laboured and when I reached out to touch him, his skin felt cold and clammy.

I raised myself on to one elbow and looked him in the face. 'Do you feel like you're slipping away, honey?' I asked.

He nodded, weakly. For days he had been talking less and less, barely answering when spoken to. Now it appeared that even that effort was beyond him.

Concerned as to what the day might bring, I rang some friends from church and arranged for Natasha to spend most of the day with them, playing with their little girl. When Maureen came by to collect Natasha later in the morning, I was in the process of trying to move Phil into the living-room, where I had opened up the sofa-bed.

'Here, let me help,' she said, getting alongside him so that we could lie him down.

'It's washday,' I explained, panting slightly with exertion. 'Our bedroom's too far away from the living-room for me to keep an eye on him. He's better off here while I do the ironing.'

When Maureen left with Tash in tow, I sat beside Phil and put my hand on his forehead. His complexion was paler than ever and I was sure that the end could not be long. I rang our pastor, Derek.

'Could I take you up on your offer to sit with Phil?' I asked. 'I need to slip out to do some shopping.'

When I returned – and after Derek had left – I tried to get Phil to drink something: first his protein drink, Meritene; then a bottle of Fanta; and finally some water. Virtually nothing had passed his lips all day and I was so alarmed when my efforts were unsuccessful that I rang Dr Hirschel.

'I'll come straight away,' he said and true to his word, he arrived before noon.

He put a hand on Phil's forehead and looked in his eyes, then he pinched the skin on Phil's arm to measure the elasticity. When it failed to spring back and simply remained in a grey fold, he turned to me.

'He's very dehydrated,' he said, quietly. 'It probably will not be long now.'

My heart was hammering. Could I cope, I wondered? But I had promised Phil that I would see him through to the end and I could not back out now.

'What should I do . . . when he goes . . . ?'

Dr Hirschel's brown eyes filled with compassion. 'There's a funeral parlour near the hospital. If you like, when I get back I will send a nurse over to get some information? Yes? Then I will telephone you to let you know.'

Within the hour, the doctor rang. He gave me the telephone number and price list for the funeral parlour, and another which he told me was a 'bip' number.

'That is for you to call a doctor in to do the death certificate,' he explained.

Thanking him, I scribbled down the details, gripping the pencil hard in my hand and pressing unduly on the paper. Then I rang off and sank on to a chair.

On the far side of the room, Phil lay inert on the sofa. Half for his benefit and half for mine, I whispered: 'This is so hard.'

He gave no sign of having heard me. Outside, on the rue du Gothard traffic noise faded to a dull growl as the world went about its business. Inside – in the flat – the silence was profound.

Tearfully, I struggled with my grief.

*   *   *

Later, when the washing was finished and I had eaten a simple lunch, I sat down to watch *Dallas* as usual. Swiss television transmitted some programmes in both French and English, and following the Ewing family traumas was my relaxation each afternoon. All the while, as I watched, Phil's breathing became increasingly more laboured. A sheen of sweat covered his face, his hands lay inert and his eyes were unblinking.

At the end of my programme, I switched over to watch the *Knot's Landing* re-runs, then decided against it because Phil was never a big fan of the prime-time soaps. Briefly, it occurred to me to put some punk music on the stereo for him, but somehow, that didn't seem appropriate. Then, suddenly, I was struck with inspiration. Phil had often said that *The Planets* by Holst was one of his favourite discs, and I knew that the Jupiter movement could touch him like nothing else. I set up the stereo then fast-forwarded until the amplifier picked up the familiar theme.

Music poured into the room, swelling and receding like waves on the sand. I glanced at Phil to gauge its effect. It was a fitting piece: not Mars, Bringer of War, for the war that had raged in Phil's body in the last few years was now almost vanquished; nor Saturn, Bringer of Old Age, for that had been denied him; nor even Venus, Bringer of Peace, nor Mercury the Winged Messenger – though either would have been apt.

No. There was only Jupiter that was capable of expressing the nature of this man, for whom life had spelled fun, and whose humour was appreciated by so many. Jupiter. Bringer of Jollity. This was the right and proper herald for Phil: ushering his being through the doors of death; announcing his arrival at the threshold of Life.

I sat down on the sofa-bed and took Phil's left hand in mine. It felt cool and damp. Still he neither moved nor blinked and he appeared to be unaware of my presence. I doubted that he was conscious.

Even so, I leaned forward and whispered, close to his ear. 'I'm ready for you to go when you want, honey. I'll try and teach Tash about cricket as best I can. I love you. And I'll miss you.'

There was no response, no flicker of recognition. Gradually, his breathing got lighter. All the while I kept hold of his hand, sometimes stroking, sometimes squeezing gently. And all the while, I whispered into his ear.

Some time in the middle of the afternoon, Phil's breathing stopped. I checked the clock. It was three-forty. Reaching forward, I slipped a hand under his T-shirt, pressed my palm on his chest and felt for a heartbeat. For some moments, I was unsure if he had truly gone. It was difficult to tell. My heart pounded. And my pulse surged: a loud rush in my ears.

This was no good. I had to be certain – could not ring the doctor till I was. I got up and went first to my bedroom for a mirror; then, as an afterthought, to Natasha's room – for her toy stethoscope. I held the mirror to Phil's mouth and nose, and looked for the tell-tale sign of misting. There was none. Then with Tash's 'scope in my ears, I listened for a heartbeat. Nothing.

I wiped a hand across my face. My eyes and cheeks felt moist. Yet there was no sense of grief. Sitting there, with Phil's body still warm to the touch, I was unaware of the passing of time. Like an echo, Holst's music repeated in my ears, and my mind was filled with one image only: I could see Phil's soul, hovering inches above his inert body. He was watching me crying – just like in the movies – and I felt a rush of love and happiness. Simply to know that he was free of his body. He was on his way to heaven.

10

The Last Mountain

'He will wipe every tear from their eyes. There will be no more death or mourning or crying or pain, for the old order of things has passed away.'

Revelation 21:4

Oxford was packed with tourists that August Bank Holiday Saturday, 1991. They stood in small groups, or milled about on the narrow pavements, necks craned and cameras clicking, to take in the magnificence of English Gothic architecture. St Aldate's, the church that Phil and I had attended during our years in the city, was no less an object of scrutiny. And of particular interest, it seemed, were the folk arriving for Phil's memorial service, who were subjected to the stares of onlookers – some sympathetic, others frankly curious. Under their gaze, I felt hot and uncomfortable.

Grasping Tash's hand to restrain her, I stepped into the building. The effect was immediate: like plunging into deep and tranquil waters. The heat, the glare, the hurly-burly of the street scene, and the traffic's roar, receded to a subdued thrum. Inside, enclosed by the solid mass of ancient stone walls, was a cool, timeless quality that wrapped itself around me, soothed and bathed me.

Having deposited Tash in the crèche, I joined the rest the family and walked down the aisle to the front, where the rector, David MacInnes, waited to greet us. Behind him was the altar, and behind that, pinned to the wall, a large blue banner. It read: 'Be still and know that I am God.'

There was no coffin, for Phil had been cremated in Switzerland. My parents had flown over from America for the service in Geneva, where they'd met some of the Glaxo staff. Then after a short stay, they had returned home, unable to accompany Natasha and me back to England for Phil's thanksgiving.

I'd chosen this weekend for the event, in collaboration with his mum and dad, because of the Bank Holiday and was gratified to see so many familiar faces filling the church. The Order of Service also met with my approval. This was what Phil had wanted: his express wish made to me that day back in 1990 and now faithfully executed.

'"I always give thanks for every memory of you – your faith, your hope, your love . . . "' said David MacInnes, quoting the familiar opening of many of Paul's epistles. 'Those words are easy to echo about Phil,' he continued. 'That's one of the joys of this occasion . . . '

There had never been any question in Phil's mind about where he would be going. 'When I get to heaven,' he'd always said, 'I'm going to run and jump.'

Recalling his wasted state when I'd held his hand and watched him slip away, I knew that I could never wish him back in that shell of a body. He'd been so frail at the end.

The thoughts and images crowded in, and for a few moments St Aldate's, the congregation, the music and the readings faded to the background, as I relived the events of that Friday evening, three weeks earlier.

*   *   *

The lines of pain that had etched Phil's face had softened in death and he looked perfectly at peace. I sat on, stroking his hand; whispering to him of my love for him;

my gratitude of his for me; and basking in the knowledge that Phil was with Jesus.

After a time – though it was probably only a few moments – Simonne arrived to tell me that she had collected Tash from Maureen's and would keep her for the night.

'Phil's gone,' I said, at the front door.

For a moment, Simonne looked at me blankly. Then her face streamed with a sudden onrush of tears.

'Phil's dead?' she sobbed.

She stumbled into the sitting-room and stood looking down at Phil's body. I could see her still – a tableau of grief imprinted upon my mind.

When she left a numbness took me over. I set into motion the required train of events with all the outward calm detachment of an automaton. Yet looking back now, my actions seemed veiled in a haze – of muddled phone calls, people coming and going. And all the while, Phil's body lay inert and cold.

I knew I had to get a death certificate signed, but was unable to think whom to call. The bip number was forgotten. And eventually, when only Dr Hirschel's name would come to mind, I tried him.

A stranger's voice answered, and for some moments I grappled with my French, unable to express myself properly.

'I'm afraid Dr Hirschel is unavailable,' the man said, when I at last made myself understood.

Then I remembered the *Association des Médecins*. Again, my French deserted me; but after a time, I managed to convey my situation. They promised to send someone as soon as possible. Immediately, I rang the funeral home, only to be told to call back after the death certificate had been issued, so whilst I waited, I contacted Phil's parents in England and broke the news.

The effort left me drained. And feeling in need of company and support, I rang Derek.

'Can I take you up on your offer to come over?' I asked,

and was grateful when both he and Beryl arrived to sit with me.

After what seemed an interminable delay and several more phone calls, the doctor arrived, with sincere apologies. He had witnessed an accident on the way over and consequently had had to stop and help. He gave Phil a cursory examination.

'Cause of death?' he asked in French.

Without thinking, I replied: '*À cause du SIDA.*'

Only in retrospect did I realise my omission. I had not mentioned that Phil was a haemophiliac and had been infected through Factor VIII. But then – the doctor hadn't asked!

Soon after his departure, the men from the funeral parlour arrived. They indicated that Derek, Beryl and I should leave the room whilst they dressed Phil in the grey suit, grey and white striped shirt, navy tie and boots that I had set out ready.

'I don't see Phil's wedding ring on his finger,' I said to Derek as we retreated to the bedroom.

'You don't want to lose that!' Derek replied. And he returned to the sitting-room to ask the men to look out for it.

Later, he put the plain gold band in my outstretched hand. 'Here,' he said. 'It was down the side of the sofa.'

Thanking him, I slipped it on to the ring finger of my left hand. 'I wonder if it fell off?' I murmured. 'Or whether Phil took it off to give to me?'

At last, the funeral party indicated that they had completed their job and invited me to return to the sitting-room. Tentatively, I approached the stretcher on which Phil lay. His eyes stared sightlessly upward.

One of the men spoke to me gently, in French. 'I am afraid the lids will not close.'

I nodded.

'Nor are we able to straighten the leg.'

I nodded again, wordlessly gesturing my acceptance of these facts.

'You would like to say "Goodbye", madame?'

The men turned away.

My heart thumped erratically and my mouth felt dry. I gazed at Phil. It was strange. Seeing him like this. Lying there. Dressed up. After all this time. I reached out. Touched his hand; then his cheek. Silently, I mouthed my farewell.

'Goodbye, Phil . . . '

But it wasn't Phil. And it hadn't been for weeks.

I made a sound, to indicate that I was finished. The men took up the stretcher. It was time for them to go.

Soon afterwards, I saw Derek and Beryl off, too. Made more phone calls. Went out to a nearby Italian restaurant. Ordered pasta. And ate slowly. Then I returned home.

The flat felt cold and empty. The sheets, where Phil had lain, were still spread in a crumpled fashion on the sofa-bed – together with his T-shirt. I folded them roughly, and put them in the wash. Then I straightened the room. And went to bed. Alone.

Next day, when Tash returned from Simonne's, I gently broke the news.

'Daddy's gone to be with Jesus.'

Her eyes widened. 'Oooh . . . ' she said, on a long, drawn note.

Then I drew her into my arms. And wept.

*   *   *

My Order of Service quivered before me. Tears sprang to my eyes and I blinked to disperse them. All around me voices were raised, and with them was mine. We were singing 'I cannot tell' to the lovely, haunting melody of 'Danny Boy' and I could hear Phil's voice, long ago, making his choice of music for his own thanksgiving. First this beautiful hymn of assurance, each verse beginning with an admission of the incomprehensible nature of the mighty workings of God; yet culminating in the glorious assurance of salvation. Then 'The Servant King' – a moving reminder of Jesus' humanity and humility – the Son of God who laid aside His Deity; came into the world a helpless babe; and grew to manhood intent upon serving rather than in being served; finally taking my sins upon Himself; dying in agony to pay the price of my wrongdoing, that I might be forgiven, restored. And to end the service, 'Jerusalem' – the wonderful anticipation of a green and pleasant land; an eternity spent in the Presence of God.

We finished the first hymn and were seated. Arthur Duke, a family friend, came to the lectern, spoke of Phil's childhood, his 'grit and determination' – 'a fidget, always keen to be doing.'

'Despite the limitations of his physical disabilities,' he said, 'Phil insisted on joining in volleyball, canoeing, tennis . . . and was given no quarter by the young people. He suffered, but did not whinge. And it is to his parents' credit that he was allowed to live a normal life.

'Phil,' he continued, 'had a heart for the disadvantaged.' And he recalled one boy who had repeatedly turned to Phil for help. Phil had been a supporter of Ipswich Town, Division Two, he told us, and was also a keen mountaineer. 'As far as Phil was concerned,' he said, 'a mountain was there to be conquered. The top was his goal.'

I glanced at Dad. Caught his eye. And smiled briefly.

A reading from Ecclesiastes 3:1–13 followed; and another song. Then Mark Cassidy, Phil's friend from Birmingham University, read a poem that he had written for the occasion.

I remember covering each other's absence
from laboratory practicals.
Myself away at union meetings,
while you'd gone to the movies.
A perfect working relationship –
when we were young together.

I remember your disbelief
when told I couldn't ride a bike;
and your insistence that I learn
on your boneshaker with the dubious brakes –
when we were young together.

I remember shopping trolleys;
how we moved house with belongings
piled high in a caravan of them;
and how you used to ride one around the
    supermarket,
in amongst the tinned tomatoes
and widest affordable selection of breakfast cereals –
when we were young together.

I remember being out in the snow at night;
hurling snowballs, making angels, and tobogganing
on borrowed lab trays and a plastic toilet lid;
crashing into drifts and each other,
and staggering, sodden, home –
when we were young together.

I remember, I remember
when we were young together.
Seeing half a dozen films in a day –
everything from the sublime to the ridiculous –
and then discussing our own scenarios into the early
    hours.
Taking the late night bus into town
in our anti-fashion threads, and dancing ourselves
to an exhausted immobility afterwards.
Plucking up the stomach to follow you
on to the fastest, scariest whirligig.

And though you've gone ahead
to where I cannot follow now,
you're here still in my memories of
us always young together.

Mark's poem was a tribute to Phil's funloving nature, and

was reflected by other friends – Steve Watson, Richard Mason and Steve Arkinstall – all of whom spoke of his 'zest for life' and his 'macabre sense of humour'. Phil was 'a pick-up for his friends' we were told, and we were reminded of his 'humility and sensitivity'. The favoured 'red and white striped jumper' featured too, and, to everyone's amusement, we learned that it had been worn throughout the entire three days of a scientific conference in Dallas, including the official dinner. As I listened, I couldn't help but reflect that heaven must be a jollier place, since Phil's arrival there.

If Phil's time on earth had been a witness to others of the Life Abundant that Jesus promises, so, too was his death. Phil had met his Maker with dignity and confidence. And he had left behind a legacy: a daughter; friends; happy memories; the book we had worked on together.

I could harbour no regrets. In marrying Phil I had had the right husband for me: a man who loved me and put me second in his life, only after God. He'd shown infinite patience with my moodiness and had helped me to grow spiritually. We had complemented one another in our interests and sense of humour, and had learned – gradually – how to communicate about the things that were important. We'd become one – but in the process had never ceased to be individuals. And of all that we had given to each other, perhaps the most precious gift had been the freedom to be ourselves.

'Thirty-four years wasn't much,' David MacInnes said of Phil, in conclusion. 'But it was enough.'

I could echo that. The life that Phil and I had led in latter years could never be said to be 'normal'. But we'd had the opportunity to enjoy each other; to grow in stature; and to make a lasting memory. Seven years of marriage wasn't long, I thought as the memorial service drew to a close. But in the end – it was enough.

*　　*　　*

'Have you thought what you'll do now, dear?' Dad asked me a day or two later.

'Well, there's the book,' I replied.

Prior to Phil's death I had sent copies of tapes and diary entries to the publishers, and subsequently, had been to see them. Their enthusiasm had amazed me, inspiring me with an ongoing sense of purpose.

'I think Dad means in the longterm, Jana,' Mum explained.

'Right,' I said. 'I'd like to return to Geneva to see out the two years in Switzerland. I think I need that sense of completion. Of feeling that I've experienced everything life has to offer in the country. And that I've come full circle.'

'That would take you to December,' Mum said. 'Will you come home to spend Christmas with us?'

'That would be nice,' I replied.

'And what then, dear?' Dad asked. 'Are you planning to go back at all?'

I shook my head. 'It wouldn't be financially viable for me to stay on in Switzerland,' I said. 'I'd like to settle somewhere nearby, if that's okay, so Tash could grow up knowing her grandma and grampa. Then I suppose I'll have to think about finding a job.'

'You'll have the money from the MacFarlane Trust,' Dad reminded me. 'Invested wisely, that could bring in a small income.'

In the early days, after Phil's pneumocystis in 1987, I had often wondered what the future would hold. Sometimes, returning from Tesco, with Natasha in her pushchair, I'd find myself walking along weighing up the job opportunities that would be open to me. Now, suddenly, such prospects looked brighter.

When we had first moved to Geneva in January 1990 and Phil had been forced to return temporarily to the UK for hospital treatment, his father had told him of litigation being taken against the British Government. Suits were to be filed on behalf of haemophiliacs who had contracted AIDS as a result of infected Factor VIII, in pursuit of compensation for them and their families. Each case was to be heard individually.

Dad had come across this information quite by accident whilst attending a medical himself and, urged by his doctor, he had advised Phil to apply for his name to go forward on the writ. There had been no way in which we could have afforded the costs, nor were we eligible for legal aid. However, Dad had offered to pay and we had just made the deadline for filing.

Apart from the occasional questionnaire and numerous letters keeping us informed of the situation, we had all but forgotten the proceedings. However, one important fact had emerged. It seemed that Phil's case rested on whether or not he had been infected whilst still in Britain or during the two years he had lived and worked in America. Obviously, the British Government would not hold itself responsible for infection resulting from blood that had not been imported by them from the States.

By what could only be called one of God's 'coincidences', within days of arriving in America, Phil had had a blood sample taken by a doctor in the Department of Haematology in the Medical College of Virginia. Again, by some quirk of Divine Providence – for it was not normal practice – that doctor had kept the sample and, amongst others, had subsequently tested it for the AIDS virus. Moreover, he had shown Phil a copy of the test report, demonstrating quite categorically, that Phil had been infected prior to his trip to America. On the basis of this document, Phil's claim was proven, though ultimately, the cases were never actually heard in court.

In November 1987, through the Haemophilia Society, the British Government had made a £10 million grant available to help haemophiliacs who were HIV positive. The fund was administered by the MacFarlane Trust, which had been set up on 10th March, 1987 especially for the purpose, and it had been stipulated that payments were to be made on the basis of need, rather than as compensation. These took the form of regular weekly payments to haemophiliacs registered with the Trust, to enable them to cope with the extra costs of living with the HIV virus. In addition, single grants were made available for individual specific needs. Under this last heading, we had received £875 towards the cost of our holiday in July, 1990; £100 for a commode; and a similar sum for extra bedding.

By 23rd November, 1989 an additional grant of £24 million had been made available by the government in order that *ex gratia* payments of £20,000 could be paid to every eligible haemophiliac, or to their dependants. Accordingly, a new Discretionary Trust had been set up by the MacFarlane Committee, for the purpose of its administration and distribution, and in February 1990, this sum had been deposited in our Jersey bank account.

Finally, towards the end of 1990, the government had announced that it was prepared to make a settlement to litigants and their families. On 7th May, 1991, a further £42 million had been paid to the Trust and I had learned that, as a widow with a dependent child, I was eligible for a small pension of £15 per week, plus a lump sum of £60,500 in addition to the £20,000 already received.

With careful investment, and with an income from the house in Percy Street, I would have a breathing space before having to find employment. Moreover, I realised that the cushioning effect of this money could open up further opportunities. Should I wish to, I could go back to university to obtain a degree in Speech Therapy. Then I would be qualified to practise. Slowly, the idea began to take shape. And suddenly, the future appeared less bleak.

It seemed that I had something to look forward to, after all.

* * *

Early in September, I returned to Geneva to see out the two years I had promised myself. Natasha accepted

Phil's absence with equanimity, speaking of him often, and telling everyone, with great alacrity, that her daddy had gone to be with Jesus.

Shortly before Christmas, we said farewell to our friends, packed up our belongings and returned to England for good. For some months we lived with Phil's family at Sevenoaks, then in March, after the death of his Gran, we moved into her flat.

Everyone who knew me had commented on my strength and composure. I missed Phil, yet I felt that I had done my grieving prior to his death and had no need to do so again. God was my strength and God my fortress. The quiet assurance that had possessed me for so long was evident in the way in which opportunities opened up. By April 1992, I was well established in a part-time job in a local coffee-shop run by Christians; was actively involved in Vine Evangelical Church, and had been accepted at two universities. Tash, too, had settled down to life in England and was happily integrated at a nearby school.

There remained only one task to be accomplished; one last wish of Phil's to be carried out; one final 'laying to rest' of his body and soul. For some time, I pushed it to the background of my thinking: a ten-inch urn, filled with his remains.

'When I'm gone,' Phil had said to me that morning long ago in Geneva, 'would you scatter my ashes on Blencathra?'

We'd visited the Fell in June 1986 when on holiday in the Lake District, and Phil had always regarded the climb to the summit as one of his most worthwhile achievements. It was fitting that this should be his ultimate resting place.

Unable to define my reluctance as anything other than vague concerns about the weather, the tourists and Tash's schooling, I knew I could delay no longer. Committing the details to God, I finally set a date. On 31st May, 1992, I left Tash in the care of her Aunty Trin, and travelled north with Phil's mum and dad.

Next day, after a night at a Travelodge near Haydock,

I woke early, and before getting out of bed, I lay quietly
thinking of Phil. Memories flooded through my mind:
the day we met; holding hands in the cinema; our first,
tentative kiss. I recalled our wedding; being carried over
the threshold of 73 Percy Street; and the feel of Phil's arms
around me as we lay in bed talking, sharing our hopes, our
aspirations. Had we truly fulfilled our marriage vows? I
believed I could say that we had. Silently, I brought the
words to mind.

> I thank God for bringing us together. I look forward
> to sharing my life with you. I pray that my heart will
> always be open to you and yours to mine. I love you
> as a friend and equal. I will not try to change you, for
> I accept you as you are. I will be honest, faithful, and
> will work with you through good times and bad, so that
> our marriage can mean for ever.

Together. For ever. Neither life nor death could separate
us from the love of God. Nor, I knew, with an absolute
certainty, from our love of one another. Lying alone in
the narrow single bed, I drew comfort from the ease with
which I could summon my recollections. And the nearness
of Phil.

Ready for the day ahead, I showered, dressed and
breakfasted with Mum and Dad. Then we loaded the car
and headed off towards Keswick in search of the footpath
we had chosen to follow. Phil had owned a complete set
of Wainwright's pocket-book guides, and I had selected
Doddick Fell for the climb to the summit because although
it was steep, it was the most direct. Dad was to accompany
me to the top whilst Mum waited below and once we
had donned hiking socks and boots, we started off up
the ridge.

Dad, who was a keen gardener, was in better shape
than I and walked a little ahead. By the time we had
crossed Scaley Beck – negotiating the stream with care
– and begun to climb the steep grassy slopes, I had to

catch my breath every fifteen to twenty steps. Alone with my thoughts, I reflected that it had always been so. In the past I had complained bitterly to Phil as I'd forced my slack muscles to respond to the pace he had set.

This was different. Though just as unfit, I was climbing with a purpose. In my knapsack, still wrapped in a plastic carrier bag, exactly as I'd received it from the funeral director, I carried the urn that contained Phil's ashes. It was heavy, but I didn't mind. It was as important to me that I get to the top as it had ever been with Phil.

Though bright, the sky was overcast. Even so, the exercise made me perspire and I was glad of the break when we stopped halfway for lunch. I mopped my brow with my T-shirt and took out my Ryvita and cheese sandwich, salad and juice.

Dad nodded at me, indicating the way my legs dangled from the ledge on which I was seated. 'A true Philip position if ever there was one,' he said. And I smiled with pleasure to think of the unconscious manner in which I had mimicked his pose.

As soon as we had finished, we pressed on. Despite a darkening sky, the summit was clearly in sight. Although we could see walkers on the other Fells, we'd encountered no one during our climb. Only a few mountain sheep and their young lifted their heads briefly to watch our ascent, then returned to cropping the short, springy turf.

We reached the top at twenty past one, and stopped to catch our breath. Two and a half hours had elapsed since we'd waved goodbye to Mum, and in that time we had climbed 2,150 feet. Haze all but obscured the view, but in the distance we could see the outline of surrounding mountains, silhouetted against the sky; and below us were the smooth glassy surfaces of the lakes that gave the area its name.

A couple were picnicking on a grassy ledge just below the summit, so Dad and I walked along the top of Blencathra towards Gategill Fell Top. Then we veered off the path until we were out of sight, took off our knapsacks and sat them on the ground. Carefully, I removed the urn and set it alongside. For a moment, Dad and I stood back, surveying our precious cargo as if it were a time bomb which we dared not touch. Then I stepped forward and pulled off the yellow and red ribbon and the official seal of the Geneva authorities.

Two screws were revealed. The lid was firmly attached to the base! And there had been no way of knowing until I had removed the ribbons. Helplessly, Dad and I looked at each other.

Then we burst out laughing. Tears streamed from our eyes, and we collapsed on to our knees. Peals of laughter rang round the mountain top. We laughed until we were hugging our sides, rocking back and forth on the scant wiry mountain grass.

'We remembered the urn . . . ' I gasped, 'but we never thought of this.'

'I don't think I can cope with going down for a screwdriver,' Dad spluttered. 'I'd never make it back up again.'

That sent us into fresh paroxysms of delight and as I held my aching ribs, I was sure that Phil would have enjoyed this moment.

Gradually, we calmed down and considered the possibilities. I inserted my fingernail into the groove of one of the screws, and attempted to turn it. I was unsuccessful and was rewarded only with a ripped-off nail. When the zip from my haversack proved too big, I stood up and looked around. There were a number of walkers besides the picnicking couple and reluctantly, I decided that there was no alternative but to approach them for help.

'I suppose I'll have to ask if anyone has a screwdriver,' I said. 'But I'm not keen on having to explain why.'

When I turned back, however, Dad had managed to shift one of the screws with his zip and was already tackling the second.

Once the screws were removed from the urn, I lifted off the lid. Inside was a white plastic bag, tied with a gold wire. I untwisted it and looked inside. I had expected to see fine black ash and found it difficult to reconcile the greyish-white gravel that was revealed with all that remained of the man I loved.

'It seems funny to think that this was Phil,' I said.

'But it isn't Phil now,' Dad replied, gently.

No, I thought. It isn't Phil now. This ash was a dead thing. But Phil's soul would never die. I'd had that assurance since the day of his passing. Though his mortal body was no more, Phil would live on. The essential part of him – that which made him uniquely himself – was, even now, safe in the presence of God. My confidence rested, not in the person that Phil was – wonderful, kind and spiritual though he'd been. No! My conviction lay in the person that Jesus is: God's own Son, sent from heaven to earth, to show by His life the love of the Father, and to show by His death that He was the Way. The Way to forgiveness. The Way to new Life.

Having once seen a film where a woman had been covered in the ashes she was scattering, I first checked the wind direction, then reached into the bag and grasped a handful of Phil's remains. Facing north, I flung it into the breeze. White particles settled on to the ground, starkly visible against the dark earth. Over and over, I repeated the action, until the bag was nearly empty. Then I waved it in the air to be sure that nothing remained.

Dad stood by and watched, and took a few photographs with my camera. I was grateful for his insight. I would have felt awkward asking. When I had finished, he said, 'Shall we pray?'

We squatted down, clasped hands and closed our eyes.

'Lord, we want to thank you for Philip's life,' Dad began. 'He was a good husband, father and son. We thank you that he is now happy with you. We especially want to thank you for being with us today, in our climb, and in our fulfilling this last request. We think now of the future and ask that you be close to Jana and Natasha. Lord, in all these things, we praise you. Amen.'

'Amen,' I echoed.

As Dad was finishing, I felt the first drops of rain. I'd prayed for good weather, and God had granted my request. Now it seemed fitting that He should let us feel His touch in this way.

'That was very good. Quite positive,' Dad said. I agreed. I felt the satisfaction of a job well done, the fulfilment of Phil's last request.

Dad picked up his knapsack. 'Shall we go?'

We started down from the top, and decided to return via Scales Fell, a gentler grassy slope than our ascent. Fifteen minutes later, I turned and looked back. The summit was obscured. Shrouded in mist. And the rain began to fall in earnest. It would be washing Phil's ashes into the soil, I thought, blending his remains into Blencathra, the mountain he loved, so that he and it would be one. He had reached the pinnacle. Had climbed his last mountain. And knowing that, I felt at peace.

APPENDIX

A good deal of ignorance and hysteria still surrounds the subject of AIDS and, despite ongoing research, medical and scientific data is unable, categorically, to refute some of society's deepest fears. Besides, in an attempt to alert people to the real dangers of the disease, there may be a tendency on the part of those 'in the know', to act the Bogeyman and to encourage, rather than lessen those fears.

Inevitably, therefore, some of the readers of this book may be alarmed by – perhaps even critical of – certain decisions and events described in its pages. And at the end of the day, it has to be said that some of those decisions will have been taken in an entirely subjective manner. In the same way, advice given to the individuals concerned may have depended very much upon their own, particular circumstances.

Certain facts, however, are indisputable. HIV is a virus which destroys three types of cells in the body: the lymphocyte, the macrophage, and the neurological cell. Disease of these cell types is responsible for immune deficiency, diarrhoea and wasting, and brain disease, respectively. Obviously, the immune deficiency renders the patient vulnerable to infections which would otherwise be successfully fought.

Secondly, despite being classified as an 'infectious disease', the Human Immunodeficiency Virus (which may, or may not develop into AIDS) is not easily communicable.

The virus can be transmitted from person to person by sexual intercourse, or by direct inoculation in to the bloodstream. It is not transmitted by normal domestic contact.

Sensible precautions, such as the wearing of rubber gloves by those treating the patient, are, therefore, all that is necessary when dealing with infected products such as soiled dressings or linen. Clothing and bedding can be washed in the usual way in the domestic wash without fear of contamination, although in the case of laundry soiled by blood or body wastes, it may be advisable to wash these separately at the highest possible temperature setting.

The virus is, actually, extremely short-lived once outside the body. Sanitary towels, tampons and dressings for wounds, as well as colostomy bags and their contents, may safely be disposed of via a flushing lavatory, or by incineration as appropriate. Routine cleansing of surfaces and soiled articles can adequately be dealt with by the use of normal household bleaches such as Domestos, which instantly destroy the virus.

It therefore follows that, providing these guidelines are adhered to, risk from a particular source to the general public is negligible, even where amenities are shared. Although companies and corporations may have a policy governing their dealings with personnel who are known to be HIV positive, the danger of infection being passed on is virtually nil. Ignorance remains the greatest enemy.

Dr TIM PETO
BM, BCh, MA, DPhil, FRCP
Consultant Physician in Infectious Diseases
Oxfordshire Health Authority.